Sustainable Investment Policy Perspectives in the Southern African Development Community

OECD
BETTER POLICIES FOR BETTER LIVES

Please cite this publication as:
OECD (2023), *Sustainable Investment Policy Perspectives in the Southern African Development Community*, OECD Publishing, Paris, https://doi.org/10.1787/02c9ef1d-en.

ISBN 978-92-64-32980-5 (print)
ISBN 978-92-64-54621-9 (pdf)
ISBN 978-92-64-43565-0 (HTML)
ISBN 978-92-64-68776-9 (epub)

Photo credits: Cover © athenailya/Getty Images

Corrigenda to OECD publications may be found on line at: www.oecd.org/about/publishing/corrigenda.htm.

Foreword

The recent African Continental Free Trade Agreement (AfCFTA) and its related Protocols will offer greater investment opportunities for SADC Members within an integrated continental market as well as increased competition for footloose investment. This implies an even greater need to focus on raising the competitiveness of the region for sustainable investment.

The Investment Division of the OECD Secretariat has been working closely with the SADC Investment Sub-Committee for over a decade to improve the investment climate across the region and within individual countries through OECD *Investment Policy Reviews*. Most recently, the OECD has collaborated with the World Bank to develop a SADC Investment Climate Scorecard. The first phase of this project involved the addition of SADC Member States to the OECD *FDI Regulatory Restrictiveness Index*, a key measure of the extent of discrimination covering over 100 countries worldwide.

This report introduces newly developed OECD tools and analysis to the SADC region, including both FDI Qualities and a database on investment incentives. It is designed as a baseline diagnostic to explore ways to reinvigorate the reform of the SADC investment climate in order to prepare the region for the AfCFTA, while also providing a greater focus on how to improve sustainable outcomes from investment.

The policy areas covered in this study include the national regulatory framework encapsulated in national investment laws and how this compares with initiatives at a regional level, investment promotion and facilitation in SADC, investment incentives, investment for green growth and, lastly, responsible business conduct. The selection of areas builds on OECD work in these areas to highlight essential elements of a conducive investment climate which promotes not only FDI but also sustainable development. The aim is not to provide a ready-made reform agenda for countries in the region but rather to explore policy areas which influence investment and its impact.

A companion report was also prepared for Economic Community of West African States (ECOWAS), another important regional economic community in Africa. Given that the two regions are confronted with similar challenges in mobilising investment for sustainable development, as well as in fostering greater regional and continental integration, the two reports share a similar structure and analysis. Many of the recommendations are also common, given the parallel challenges and the high level of generality of this preliminary scoping report. These reports provide a solid basis for developing a long-term programme of collaboration with each region, using more tailor-made approaches based on the specificities of each region.

This report was presented at the SADC Investment Sub-Committee meeting on 29-31 May 2023 in Victoria Falls, Zimbabwe.

Table of contents

FIGURES

TABLES

Follow OECD Publications on:

https://twitter.com/OECD

https://www.facebook.com/theOECD

https://www.linkedin.com/company/organisation-eco-cooperation-development-organisation-cooperation-developpement-eco/

https://www.youtube.com/user/OECDiLibrary

https://www.oecd.org/newsletters/

Executive summary

The Southern African Development Community (SADC) is a large and dynamic regional economic community that has been at the forefront of regional investment policymaking in Africa, with the Finance and Investment Protocol, the Investment Policy Framework, and the SADC Model Bilateral Investment Treaty. More recently, SADC Member States have worked to implement these frameworks at the national level through the National Action Programmes for Investment.

At the same time, like much of Africa, SADC faces difficulties in attracting foreign direct investment (FDI) which can contribute to sustainable development in the region. FDI flows into SADC have been volatile over the last decade, and concentrated in extractive industries, predominantly in countries with abundant fossil fuel and mineral resources. Job creation from these capital-intensive industries has been moderate, but there is evidence that foreign investors contribute significantly to innovation capacity and skills development in the region. Moreover, in recent years there has been a considerable surge in FDI in renewable energy technologies in SADC.

Attracting investment and reaping the maximum benefit in terms of sustainability depend first and foremost on the overall policy framework in which investment occurs. Policymakers need to maintain a sound, transparent and open investment climate, and adopt policies that ensure the benefits of FDI are maximised and their potential harm on the local economy, society and environment are minimised. Furthermore, targeted promotion tools and measures to enable responsible business conduct (RBC) are equally important for a sustainable investment framework.

This requires whole-of-government efforts, evidence-based policy-making and meaningful stakeholder consultations. This report looks primarily at what host governments can do to attract sustainable investment and promote the benefits of investment for social and environmental objectives, including how to facilitate and enable RBC. It provides an analysis to make SADC a preferred destination for national and foreign investment that is reinforced by effective governance that promotes sustainable and inclusive regional economic development. It is based on the OECD tools, including the Policy Framework for Investment and the FDI Qualities Policy Toolkit and Indicators. Key messages and main considerations that emerge from the report are the following:

- *Increase coherence between national legislation and regional and continental treaties.* Greater coherence in approaches within and across regions in Africa at all levels could contribute to improved clarity and predictability for both governments and investors, although sufficient room should be left for further experimentation at national level
- *Consider further integrating SDG considerations into investment promotion strategies of SADC Member States* and develop IPAs' value propositions for sustainable investment opportunities accordingly. More targeted investment generation can also allow SADC agencies to select FDI projects that are more likely to contribute to the SDGs, including by prioritising investors with good sustainability track-records.
- *Put in place adequate KPIs to select priority investors and measure their sustainability impacts.* SADC IPAs should also ensure that the KPIs used to select priority investments and measure their

outcomes are aligned with national development objectives and the agencies' overarching investment promotion priorities.

- *Use the SDGs to guide IPA aftercare services to existing investors who wish to expand or reinvest.* IPAs in SADC could consider focusing aftercare activities on those investors with the highest sustainability impacts, and take advantage of these services to better promote responsible business conduct.
- *Assess whether investment tax incentives are aligned with investment promotion strategies and sustainable development goals, and whether they are the best policy instrument to achieve these goals.* Economic, social and environmental goals might be better supported by regulations or other policies, and tax incentives should be used in complement with wider development strategies.
- *Design incentives to generate investments and related outcomes that would not materialise otherwise.* Improving incentive design, by promoting desired outcomes through tax relief on qualifying expenditure, can help limit redundancies and encourage positive spillovers.
- *Improve monitoring of tax incentive uptake and costs, and evaluation of costs and benefits of policies.* The SADC Secretariat can continue to advocate for improved monitoring and evaluation, including by supporting use of the recently reviewed SADC Tax Expenditure Model for Tax Incentives, and by further advancing cooperation on commitments related to incentives under the Protocol for Finance and Investment.
- *Strengthen NDC targets and develop long-term low-emission development strategies.* Long-term strategies provide a pathway to a whole-of-society transformation and a vital link between shorter-term NDCs and the long-term objectives of the Paris Agreement. These strategies offer many benefits, including guiding countries to avoid costly investments in high-emissions technologies, supporting just and equitable transitions, and sending early and predictable signals to investors about envisaged long-term societal changes.
- *Use SADC as a platform to promote strategic environmental assessments (SEA) and transboundary environmental impact assessment (EIA).* Recognition of transboundary SEA and EIA at the SADC level could encourage other SADC governments to adopt these tools in their national EIA systems.
- *Consider phasing out fossil fuel subsidies and using freed up funds to mitigate adverse social impacts of climate policies.* Overall, fossil fuels remain highly subsidised in Southern Africa. Phasing out subsidies could free up public funds for targeted support to ensure vulnerable groups access clean and affordable energy, but adequate compensation and support measures for those affected by subsidy reform should be put in place.
- *Increase awareness and understanding of Responsible Business Conduct (RBC).* SADC and its Member States can strategically enhance awareness of stakeholders on the importance of RBC in relation to trade and investment, through capacity-building activities and workshops on international RBC frameworks and risk-based due diligence.
- *Strengthen the domestic policy framework governing RBC.* There is still a lack of comprehensive domestic regulations and specific action plans pertaining to RBC in the region. SADC governments can take the lead by developing and implementing National Action Plans on RBC, as well as sector-specific or issue-specific reforms.
- *Ensure policy coherence and harmonisation in line with international RBC standards.* SADC serves as a platform for promoting policy coherence and harmonisation and can take further steps to achieve strong alignment and coordination of RBC policies among its Member States, ensuring a unified approach and a level playing field at the regional level.

1 Overview

This chapter provides an overview of recent foreign direct investment (FDI) trends in SADC, including a preliminary assessment of its contribution to sustainable development. It then summarises key messages and main considerations that emerge from the substantive chapters of the report.

Introduction

The Southern African Development Community (SADC) is a large and dynamic regional economic community (REC) with the second highest level of regional integration among all African RECs. It has also been at the forefront of regional investment policy making in Africa, with the Finance and Investment Protocol and the Investment Policy Framework (building on the OECD Policy Framework for Investment), as well as the SADC Model Bilateral Investment Treaty. More recently, SADC Member States have worked to implement these frameworks at country level through the National Action Programmes for Investment. At the same time, like much of Africa, SADC faces difficulties in attracting foreign direct investment which can contribute to sustainable development in the region.

The recent African Continental Free Trade Agreement (AfCFTA) and its related Protocols will offer both greater investment opportunities for SADC Members within an integrated continental market as well as increased competition for footloose investment. This will imply an even greater need to focus on raising the competitiveness of the region for investment, and on how to improve sustainable outcomes from investment.

This report introduces newly developed OECD tools and analysis to the SADC region, including both FDI Qualities and a database on investment incentives. It is designed as a baseline diagnostic to explore ways to reinvigorate the reform of the SADC investment climate in order to prepare the region for the AfCFTA, while also providing a greater focus on how to improve sustainable outcomes from investment. The policy areas covered in this study include the national regulatory framework encapsulated in national investment laws and how this compares with initiatives at a regional level, investment promotion and facilitation in SADC, investment incentives, investment for green growth and, lastly, responsible business conduct.

Recent trends in FDI in SADC and estimates of its impact

Foreign direct investment flows into the SADC region have been volatile over the last decade, exhibiting a considerable drop in 2015, and a spike in 2021 as a result of a large one-off intra-firm financial transaction in South Africa (Figure 1.1). Within the region, inward FDI stocks are highest in South Africa (51%), the largest and most diversified economy, followed by other large SADC economies that are rich in natural resources like Mozambique (15%), DR Congo (9%), and Zambia (6%). Fluctuating flows into these large recipients, combined with divestment in Angola, drove the volatile FDI performance observed in recent years. The economic importance of FDI stock relative to GDP is high, averaging 70% across the region; yet there is considerable variation across countries, with FDI shares in GDP around 10% in Comoros and Malawi, and over 250% in Seychelles and Mozambique.

New FDI projects or expansions of existing FDI projects (i.e. greenfield FDI flows) have similarly exhibited considerable volatility over the last two decades, with the value of investments flowing into the region oscillating between USD 10 and 40 billion (Figure 1.2, Panel A). The COVID-19 pandemic appeared to have a modest and transitory effect on FDI inflows into SADC, which were already low in 2019, and rose significantly above pre-pandemic levels by 2022. While the value of greenfield investments exhibits a relatively constant trend, the volume of investments has declined over the last 15 years, suggesting that SADC attracts fewer but larger investments. Jobs created from these investment projects have also been on a declining trend since 2007, suggesting that FDI inflows have become relatively more capital-intensive. A closer look at the stock of greenfield investment projects by sector shows that the vast majority of these investment are in capital-intensive sectors like coal, oil and gas (29%), metals (17%), construction (11%) and renewable energy (10%). Indeed, extraction, manufacturing, and electricity generation in the energy and metals sectors accounts for 55% of the entire stock of greenfield FDI in the region.

Figure 1.1. FDI flows into SADC has been volatile

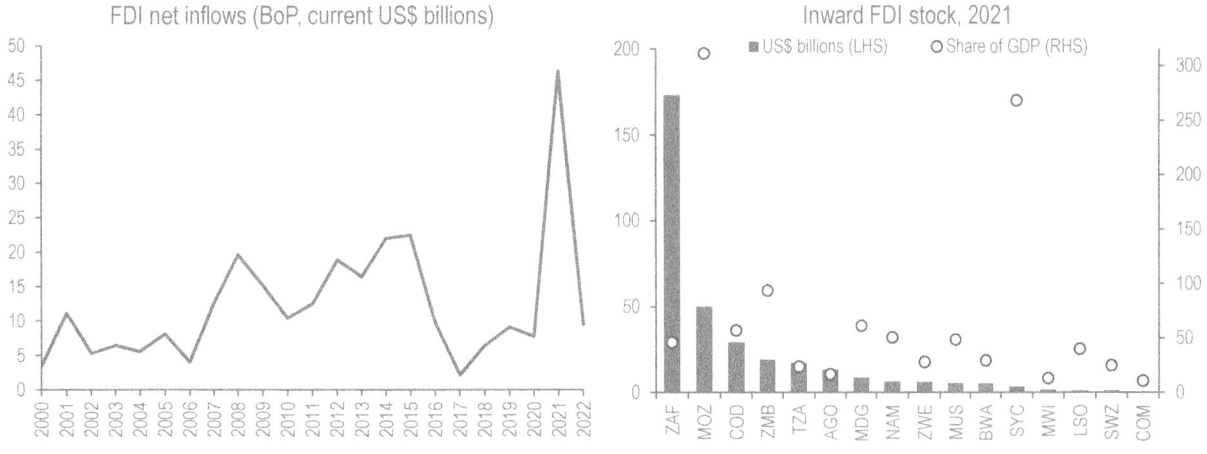

Note: The surge in inflows in 2021 is driven by one large inter-firm transaction in South Africa.
Source: OECD elaboration based on IMF (2022) Balance of Payments Statistics and UNCTAD (2023[1]).

Figure 1.2. Greenfield FDI projects have become increasingly large and capital intensive

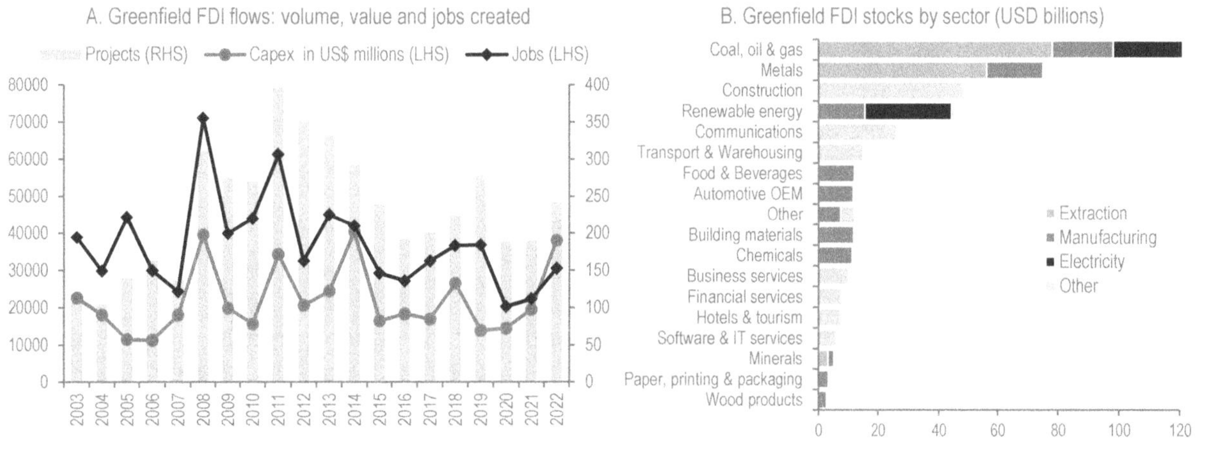

Note: Data includes all open and announced projects between 2003 and 2022.
Source: OECD elaboration based on Financial Times fDi Markets (2023[2]).

At the country-level, a similar pattern emerges (Figure 1.3). Greenfield FDI in SADC created 1.8 jobs per million USD invested, on average, well below the world average of 3.3, yet with wide variation across the region (OECD, 2022[3]). Countries with abundant natural resources, like Angola and Mozambique, attracted over two-thirds of FDI in extraction, electricity generation and construction, which are highly capital-intensive activities and exhibit the lowest job-intensity, averaging 0.8 and 1.1 jobs per million USD invested, respectively. Malawi and Seychelles also attracted considerable FDI in energy and construction activities with low job-intensity, while more diversified economies like Botswana and Mauritius attracted more labour-intensive FDI in manufacturing and services, respectively. Lesotho and Eswatini attracted the bulk of their inward FDI in garments manufacturing and food processing, and exhibit the highest job-intensity of FDI, with four and seven direct jobs created per million USD invested, respectively.

Figure 1.3. FDI-induced job creation varies according to its sectoral distribution

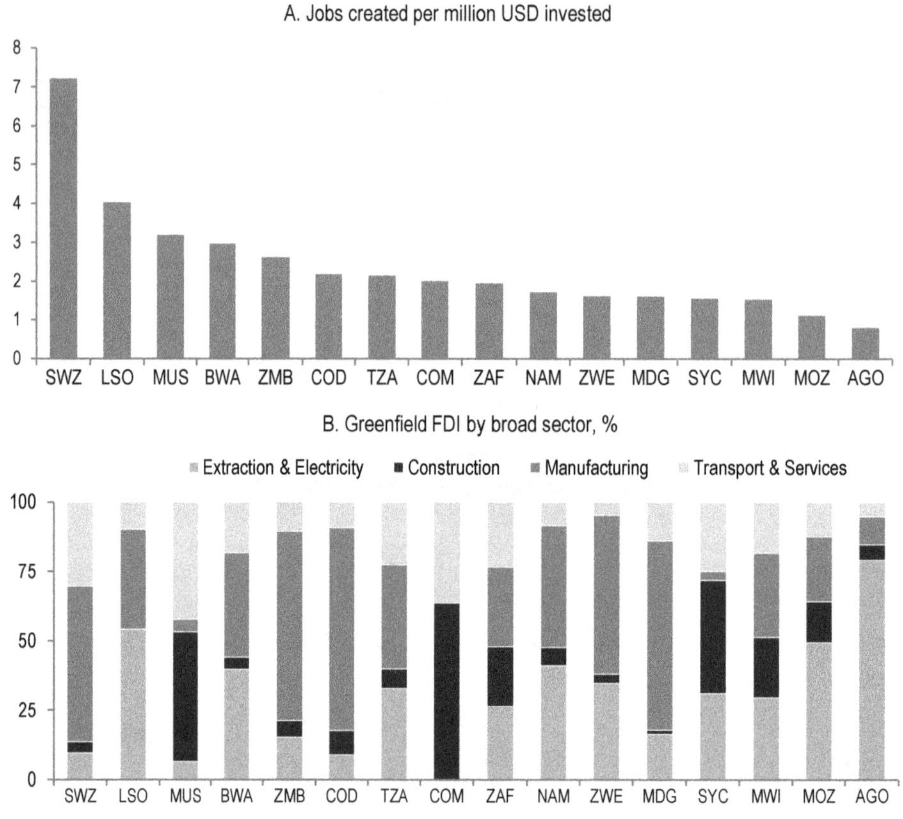

Note: The figures include all opened and announced greenfield FDI projects across SADC members between 20 003 and 2022.
Source: OECD elaboration based on Financial Times fDi Markets (2023[2]).

In light of the previous discussion, South Africa attracted 32% of the value of greenfield FDI projects in SADC while resource-rich economies jointly attracted 52%, and the remaining SADC economies attracted 16% (Figure 1.4). Among resource-rich countries, the main recipients of greenfield investments are Angola (20%) and Mozambique (15%), followed by Zimbabwe (7%), Zambia (6%) and Tanzania (6%). The largest source of greenfield investments in SADC over the last two decades is the USA (13%), followed by the UK (12%). Other major investors include France (8%), China (8%) and the UAE (7%), followed by South Africa, Italy and India, which each account for another 5% of greenfield FDI stocks. Other OECD economies including Canada, Australia and Germany have sizeable stocks of SADC FDI, at around 4% each, and invest relatively more in SADC countries that are less dependent on natural resources compared to the USA and European investors. OECD countries collectively account for two-thirds of greenfield FDI in the region, while intra-regional investment from other SADC members accounted for 8%. After South Africa, Mauritius is the second largest intra-regional investor (1.3%).

There is evidence that FDI offer additional advantages beyond the contribution to capital stock and jobs, by raising total factor productivity and the efficient use of resources in host economies, and bringing new technologies, skills and business practices. In SADC, firm-level data suggests that in most SADC countries, foreign companies are more likely to introduce new products or services than their domestic counterparts (Figure 1.5, Panel A). This pattern suggests that foreign investors have greater innovation capacity and that there may be opportunities for knowledge and technology transfers to local entities. Foreign firms are also more likely to offer training opportunities to their employees, and contribute to on-the-job skills development, suggesting that FDI plays an important role in creating quality jobs and developing human capital (Figure 1.5, Panel B). The relationship between FDI and gender equality in the labour market appears less favourable. With few exceptions, foreign firms employ smaller shares of women in their workforce and are less likely to have female top managers than domestic peers (Figure 1.5, Panel C and D), as is the case also in other regions in the world (OECD, 2022[3]).

Figure 1.4. FDI flows to SADC originate from a diversified set of investors

Greenfield FDI flows to by source and destination, 2018-22

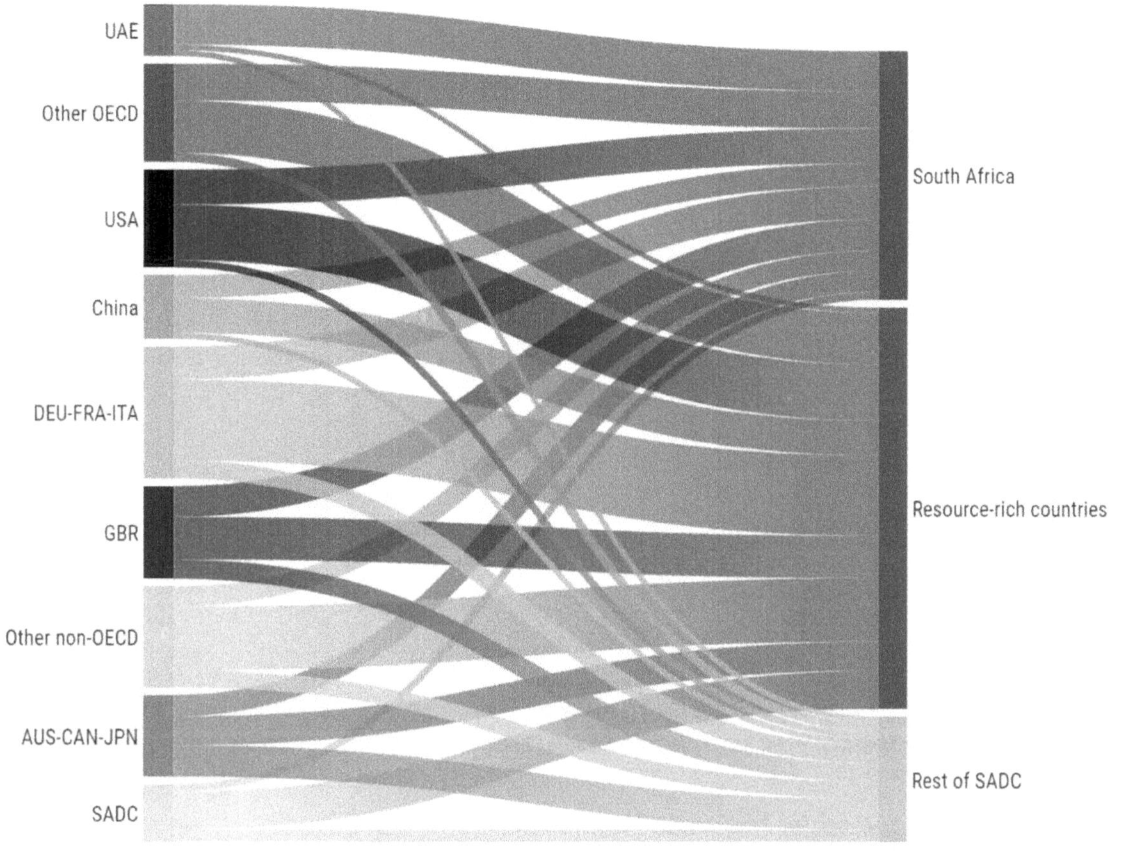

Note: The figure includes all opened and announced greenfield FDI projects over 2003 and 2022. Resource-rich countries (i.e. where natural resource rents account for at least 10% of GDP) include Angola, DR Congo, Mozambique, Zambia and Zimbabwe.
Source: OECD elaboration based on Financial Times fDi Markets (2023[2]).

FDI can make a significant contribution to the energy transition by increasing renewable energy capacity, and indeed accounts for 30% of new investments in renewable energy, globally (OECD, 2022[3]). In SADC, fossil fuels still dominate the stock of FDI in the energy sector (74%). Nevertheless, the last decade saw a fourfold increase in the stock of FDI in renewable energy compared to the previous decade, while FDI in fossil fuels shrank by 24% (Figure 1.6, Panel A). At the same time, the variation across countries remains wide (Figure 1.6, Panel B). In Angola and Mozambique, fossil fuels account for 78% and 45% of total greenfield FDI accumulated since 2003, and over 94% of FDI stocks in the energy sector. In Tanzania, Malawi, and Botswana, fossil fuels account for over a quarter of overall greenfield FDI stocks and also dwarf renewable energy FDI. Madagascar, Zimbabwe and DRC also lag behind in terms of attracting renewable energy FDI. Conversely, in Namibia, Seychelles, Lesotho and Eswatini, renewable energy FDI dominates the energy sector and has attracted a sizeable share of greenfield FDI, ranging from 10% in

Eswatini to 32% in Namibia. In Zambia and South Africa, the gap between renewable and conventional energy in terms of FDI attraction is smaller, but there is a clear trend toward greener energy.

Figure 1.5. FDI contributes to innovation capacity and skills

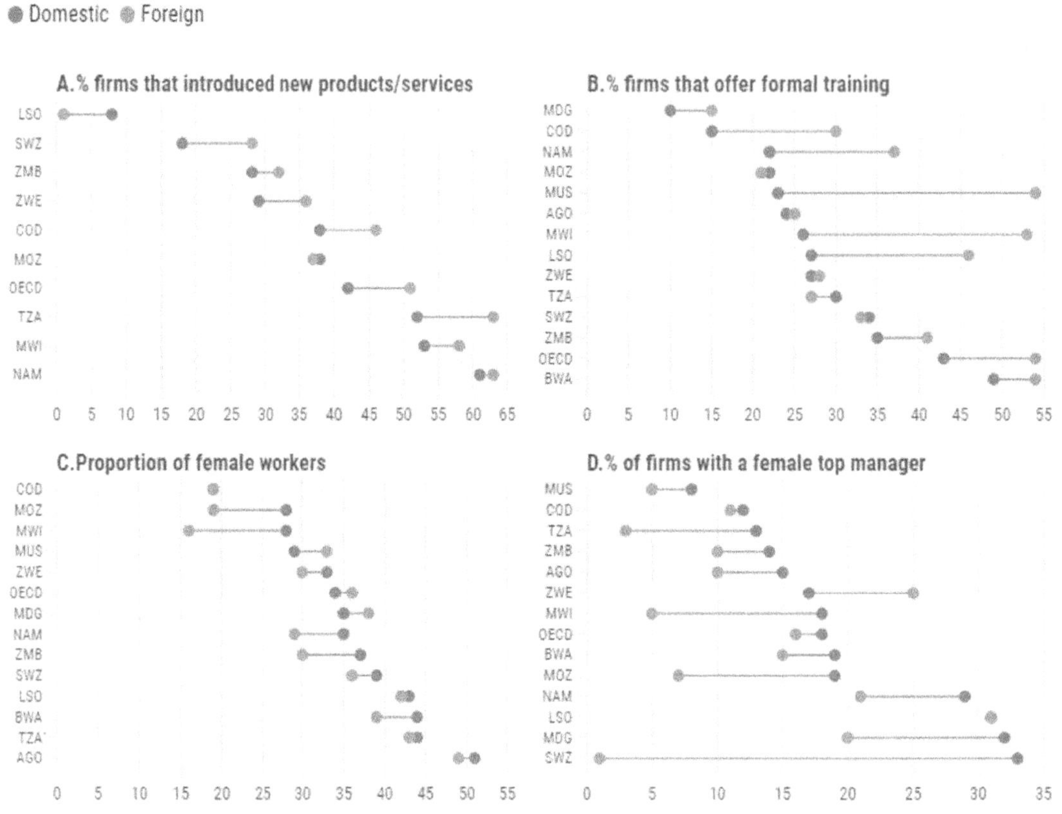

Source: OECD elaboration based on World Bank Enterprise Surveys (2022[4]).

Figure 1.6. FDI in renewables has gained momentum in the last decade

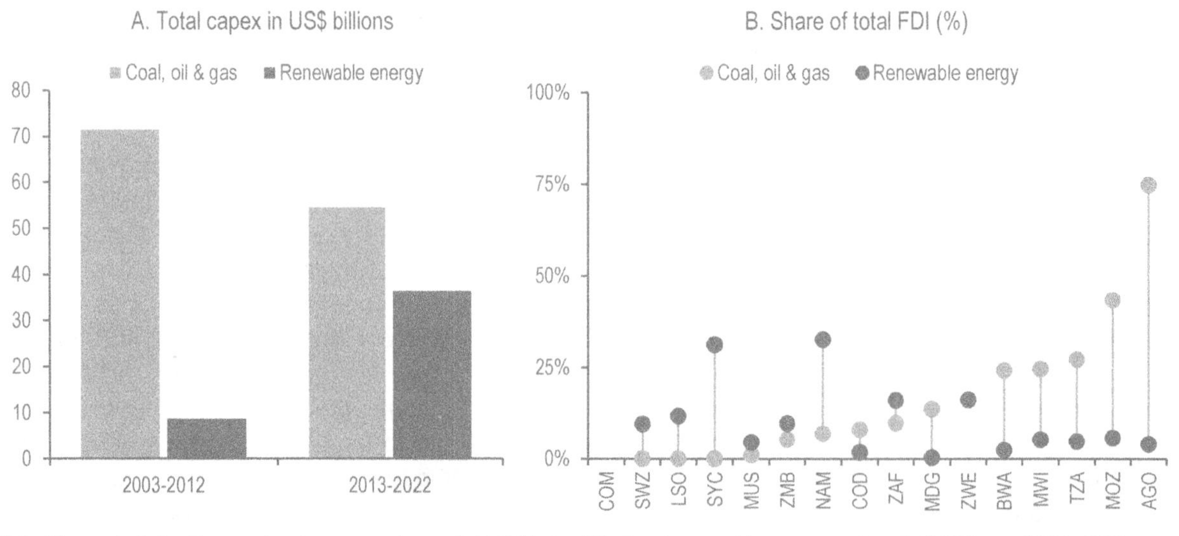

Note: Figures include all opened and announced greenfield FDI in fossil fuel and renewable energy sectors, in SADC over 203 to 2022.
Source: OECD elaboration based on FT fDi Markets (2023[2]).

Key messages and considerations

Sustainable investment has been defined as "commercially viable investment that makes a maximum contribution to the economic, social and environmental development of host countries and takes place in the framework of fair governance mechanisms" (Sauvant and Mann, 2017[9]). A broader definition would consider that sustainable investment should contribute towards achieving the Sustainable Development Goals (SDGs). While an investment project can contribute to several SDGs, trade-offs might also arise when an investment moves the host country closer to some SDGs but farther away from others.

As mentioned at the beginning of this report, the challenge for governments is not just to attract foreign investors at a time of diminishing global FDI flows, but also to ensure that the investment confers sustainable benefits on the host economy. Attracting investment and reaping the maximum benefit in terms of sustainability depend first and foremost on the overall policy framework in which investment occurs. Policymakers need to maintain a sound, transparent and open investment climate, and adopt policies that ensure the benefits of FDI are maximised and their potential harm on the local economy, society and environment are minimised. Furthermore, targeted promotion tools and measures to enable responsible business conduct (RBC) are equally important for a sustainable investment framework.

This requires whole-of-government efforts, evidence-based policy making and meaningful stakeholder consultations. This report looks primarily at what host governments can do to attract sustainable investment and promote the benefits of investment for social and environmental objectives, including how to facilitate and enable RBC. It provides an analysis to make SADC a preferred destination for national and foreign investment that is reinforced by effective governance that promotes sustainable and inclusive regional economic development. It is based on the OECD tools, including the Policy Framework for Investment and the FDI Qualities Policy Toolkit and Indicators. Key messages and main considerations that emerge from different chapters are summarised below.

Designing investment frameworks and strategies to promote sustainable investment

- *Increase coherence between national legislation and regional and continental treaties.* The analysis suggests that national investment laws do not yet fully reflect innovations at a regional or continental level, although newer investment laws seem to be closer to regional practice. Furthermore, there is still considerable diversity in individual laws across the SADC region. Greater coherence in approaches within and across regions in Africa at all levels could contribute to improved clarity and predictability for both governments and investors, although sufficient room should be left for further experimentation at national level.
- *Consider further integrating SDG considerations into investment promotion strategies of SADC Member States and develop IPAs' value propositions for sustainable investment opportunities accordingly.* Several agencies in the region have put strong focus on attracting investment in sustainable development sectors and activities, such as renewable energy, the blue economy, sustainable agriculture, forest restoration and social inclusion initiatives. The value propositions for these sustainable investment opportunities should be further developed and better marketed with stronger communication on their related incentives, industry information and legal background. More targeted investment generation can also allow SADC agencies to select FDI projects that are more likely to contribute to the SDGs, including by prioritising investors with good sustainability track-records.
- *Put in place adequate KPIs to select priority investors and measure their sustainability impacts.* While it is key to prioritise certain investments over others to respond to sustainability objectives, it is equally important to understand and track their contribution to the desired outcomes. Adopting the right KPIs is necessary to measure the results of the agency and the effective contribution of companies assisted by the IPA to sustainable development. SADC IPAs should also ensure that

the KPIs used to select priority investments and measure their outcomes are aligned with national development objectives and the agencies' overarching investment promotion priorities. Consider diversifying them to reflect all areas of the SDGs and include sustainable and inclusiveness considerations (e.g. low-carbon transition, gender equality, regional development).

- *Use the SDGs to guide IPA aftercare services to existing investors who wish to expand or reinvest.* IPAs should not only focus on promoting sustainable investment through new investments, but also use the SDGs to guide them in the way they deliver aftercare services to existing investors, not only to retain them but also to support their potential expansion or reinvestment. IPAs in SADC could, for example, consider focusing aftercare activities on those investors with the highest sustainability impacts. They could also take advantage of these services to better promote responsible business conduct within the existing business community and encourage investors to comply with sustainability-related laws more systematically, as well as to embrace responsible practices in their business operations. SADC IPAs should also consider providing more systematically matchmaking services to connect local suppliers with foreign affiliates and, as such, support the development of SMEs and sustainable local value chains

Assessing use and design of investment incentives

- *Assess whether investment tax incentives are aligned with investment promotion strategies and sustainable development goals, and whether they are the best policy instrument to achieve these goals.* SADC Member States offer a range of tax incentives to attract private investment, direct it into certain sectors and locations, and encourage certain activities. Most incentives offered in the region seek to support key sectors, notably manufacturing industries, agriculture and services. Several SADC Member States offer incentives that are fairly targeted to specific goals, including reducing the costs associated with skills training and renewable energy equipment. Yet, in some cases incentives are available to broad segments of the economy, increasing the risk of redundancy. Tax incentives are not always effective to attract investors, while tax revenues are crucial for delivering public goods and services, including those that affect the investment climate. Economic, social and environmental goals might be better supported by regulations or other policies, and tax incentives should be used in complement with wider development strategies.
- *Design incentives to generate investments and related outcomes that would not materialise otherwise.* Use of corporate-income tax exemptions is less widespread in SADC than in other regions. Most SADC countries offer primarily expenditure-based incentives (tax allowances and credits), which reduce the cost of capital. Eleven countries offer tax allowances for costs related to training, R&D, and job creation. Governments that rely more on CIT reductions and exemptions could consider phasing out most costly benefits (as Namibia has been doing since 2020) and introducing more targeted types of incentives, that reduce the cost of specific expenses (e.g. training, R&D, machinery). Improving incentive design, by promoting desired outcomes through tax relief on qualifying expenditure, can help limit redundancies and encourage positive spillovers.
- *Improve monitoring of tax incentive uptake and costs, and evaluation of costs and benefits of policies.* Better understanding of whether incentives contribute to policy goals, and at what costs, requires monitoring and evaluation. While some countries in SADC conduct tax expenditure reporting, most governments face administrative, fiscal, data and human resource constraints to carrying out in-depth evaluations. The SADC Secretariat can continue to advocate for improved monitoring and evaluation, including by supporting use of the recently reviewed SADC Tax Expenditure Model for Tax Incentives, and by further advancing co-operation on commitments related to incentives under the Protocol for Finance and Investment.

Promoting investment for green growth

- *Strengthen NDC targets and develop long-term low-emission development strategies.* Collectively SADC NDCs are not yet aligned with the objectives of the Paris Agreement. Four countries have committed to achieving net-zero GHG emissions by 2050, one by 2070, and another has already achieved is committed to maintaining net-zero. Only one country has submitted long-term strategy documents in addition to its NDCs. Ambitious long-term strategies are vital since current near-term NDCs are only sufficient to limit warming to 2.7-3.7°C. Moreover, long-term strategies provide a pathway to a whole-of-society transformation and a vital link between shorter-term NDCs and the long-term objectives of the Paris Agreement. Given the 30-year time horizon, these strategies offer many other benefits, including guiding countries to avoid costly investments in high-emissions technologies, supporting just and equitable transitions, promoting technological innovation, planning for new sustainable infrastructure in light of future climate risks, and sending early and predictable signals to investors about envisaged long-term societal changes.
- *Use SADC as a platform to promote strategic environmental assessments (SEA) and transboundary environmental impact assessment (EIA).* Southern African countries made great strides in formalising EIA into their legal frameworks, with most providing for the three critical procedural rights of access to information, public participation, and access to remedies. While most countries in the region have made SEAs a legal requirement, only three countries have developed regulations or guidelines that set out the procedures for their implementation, leaving considerable room for interpretation. Moreover, the application of EIA principles to the assessment of transboundary impacts of investment remains limited, and only one country provides a framework for the control and restriction of cross-border contamination. Recognition of transboundary SEA and EIA at the SADC level could encourage other SADC governments to adopt these tools in their national EIA systems.
- *Consider phasing out fossil fuel subsidies, and using freed up funds to mitigate adverse social impacts of climate policies.* Overall, fossil fuels remain highly subsidised in Southern Africa, with total explicit and implicit subsidies amounting to USD 62 billion in 2020, and projected to rise in subsequent years. Following the surge in fuel prices since the onset of the COVID-19 pandemic and exacerbated by the war in Ukraine, subsidy levels are set to rise with fuel prices, which may reduce government capacity to promote clean energy. Governments may resort to more targeted tools than subsidies on energy use to improve energy access and affordability. Phasing out subsidies could free up public funds for targeted support to ensure vulnerable groups access clean and affordable energy, but adequate compensation and support measures for those affected by subsidy reform should be put in place.

Promoting and enabling responsible business conduct

- *Increase awareness and understanding of Responsible Business Conduct (RBC).* Although there has been some improvement in general awareness of RBC, including international standards and expectations for due diligence, many related initiatives are still in their initial phases, and most stakeholders in the region have limited awareness regarding RBC standards and approaches to due diligence. SADC and its Member States can strategically enhance awareness of the public and private sector as well as stakeholders and foster understanding of the importance of RBC in relation to trade and investment. This may involve organising capacity-building activities and workshops on international RBC frameworks and risk-based due diligence.
- *Strengthen the domestic policy framework governing RBC*. At the regional level, SADC has established comprehensive policies that cover various areas, themes, and sectors, in relation to RBC and international RBC standards, as outlined in the SADC Investment Policy Framework. Although these frameworks serve as an initial recognition and effort to tackle RBC matters, there

is still a need for further development of SADC's policy frameworks that aim to foster and facilitate RBC. At the national level, SADC Member States have implemented a range of policies to tackle RBC concerns, and in some instances, they have begun incorporating RBC instruments into their legal systems. However, there is still a lack of comprehensive domestic regulations and specific action plans pertaining to RBC in the region. For instance, the establishment of clear expectations for due diligence has not yet been fully developed and adopted within SADC. National governments can take the lead by developing and implementing National Action Plans on RBC, as well as sector-specific or issue-specific reforms.

- *Ensure policy coherence and harmonisation in line with international RBC standards.* SADC serves as a platform for promoting coherence and harmonisation of RBC policies, aligning them with major international RBC standards notably the OECD MNE Guidelines and the OECD Due Diligence Guidance for RBC. SADC can take further steps to achieve strong alignment and co-ordination of RBC policies among its Member States, ensuring a unified approach and a level playing field at the regional level.

References

African Union (2019), *African Continental Free Trade Area Agreement*, https://au-afcfta.org/afcfta-legal-texts/. [5]

FT fDi Markets (2023), *Database of crossborder greenfield investments*, https://www.fdimarkets.com/ (accessed on 30 January 2023). [2]

OECD (2022), *FDI Qualities Indicators: 2022*, https://www.oecd.org/investment/fdi-qualities-indicators.htm. [3]

UNCTAD (2023), *Foreign direct investment: Inward and outward flows and stock, annual (Balance of Payments)*, https://unctadstat.unctad.org/wds (accessed on 30 January 2023). [1]

World Bank (2022), *World Bank Enterprise Survey*, http://www.enterprisesurveys.org/en/enterprisesurveys (accessed on 30 January 2023). [4]

2 Rebalancing and aligning investment policy for sustainable development

This chapter undertakes a baseline comparative analysis of the legal framework governing investment at the continental, regional and national levels in the Southern African Development Community (SADC). The analysis focuses on how governments in SADC are incorporating sustainability dimensions into their national treaties and domestic investment laws, as well as on the coherence between action at the national, regional and international levels.

Investment policy making today is placing greater emphasis on sustainable outcomes as part of a broader shift away from investment for its own sake and towards a more nuanced appraisal of its potential impact. As such, this new approach is generally to be welcomed, but many of the innovations are relatively recent and it is too soon to assess which provisions will have a lasting positive impact on sustainable development. The impact on attractiveness for foreign and domestic investment also remains unclear.

What is clear is that sustainable development requires both substantial investment and good regulation. The legal framework for investment comprises two levels: (i) a domestic regime involving many laws regulating market activities, often supplemented in Africa by an investment law; and (ii) international treaties that offer additional provisions and protections applicable to covered foreign investors. The international regime is in turn divided into bilateral, regional, and plurilateral approaches, including investment treaties as well as free trade agreements (FTAs) with an investment chapter.

At the international level, the new approach to sustainability can encompass several facets, from hortatory clauses in the Preamble or articles, to limitations on the scope of protections, to investor obligations. To date, concrete impact in preserving policy space has been difficult to demonstrate (OECD, 2022[1]).

A key factor in effectiveness of sustainability efforts may be regional standard-setting coupled with effective and aligned action at the domestic level. The development of regional approaches can allow a full debate with greater resources. National implementation aligned with regional approaches can increase visibility and coherence of the measures.

In Africa, sustainability dimensions are likely to become even more important once the African Continental Free Trade Area (AfCFTA) Investment Protocol is finalised. These developments will raise the issue of alignment between regional and national action. Comparing regional and national approaches to sustainable development is challenging. This chapter engages in an initial analysis to compare innovations at the regional and continental levels with the approaches embodied in national investment-related legislation within the Southern African Development Community (SADC). The analysis focuses on how governments in SADC are incorporating sustainability dimensions into their national treaties and domestic investment laws, as well as on the coherence between action at the national, regional and international levels.

The analysis below suggests that national investment laws do not yet fully reflect innovations at a regional or continental level, although newer investment laws seem to be closer to regional practice. Furthermore, there is still considerable diversity in individual laws across the SADC region. Greater coherence in approaches within and across regions in Africa at all levels could contribute to improved clarity and predictability for both governments and investors, although sufficient room should be left for further experimentation at national level.

The international regime for investment protection is under increasing strain

More than 2 500 bilateral investment treaties (BITs) and multilateral agreements with an investment chapter or provisions are in force today. Traditionally, these agreements focused on the protection of investors and investments at the post-establishment phase and had as their main goal to foster foreign investments, including by providing more legal certainty and reducing unwarranted risks for foreign investors. These international investment agreements (IIAs) constitute an important part of a country's investment framework as they offer protections and guarantees that often go beyond what is included in domestic investment laws.

IIAs typically offer covered investors substantive and procedural protection. Classic substantive standards of protection include, for instance, the protection against unlawful expropriation and against discrimination, whether between foreign and domestic investors or among foreign investors, through the National Treatment (NT) and Most-Favoured Nation (MFN) provisions. They also often cover the guarantee of fair and equitable (FET) treatment and of full protection and security (FPS), which are sometimes equated with the international minimum standard of treatment of aliens under customary international law. Lastly, they also provide a guarantee for the free transfer of funds and profits in and out of host states. From a procedural point of view, most IIAs provide for an investor-state dispute settlement (ISDS) mechanism, which allows investors to bring claims against the state in which they invested before international arbitral tribunals for an alleged breach of the IIA.

States are currently reconsidering the role, purpose and content of investment treaties, particularly the earlier generation treaties, for several reasons. Firstly, investor-state arbitration cases have risen exponentially in the past decade, including cases involving public policy or regulatory measures, with the added risk of a regulatory chill to avoid the possibility of future disputes. Secondly, academic studies have reached inconclusive results with regard to whether the treaties increase inflows of investment. Thirdly, societal demands are mounting that international investment should contribute positively to sustainable development. It is increasingly recognised that while FDI can play a crucial role in making progress toward all SDGs, particularly in advancing decarbonisation, increasing innovation, creating quality jobs, developing human capital and promoting gender equality, the effects of FDI are not always positive and impacts can differ across areas of sustainable development.

Partly as a result, some countries such as India, Indonesia and South Africa have terminated their treaties. Many other governments have worked to improve the functioning and perceived fairness of treaties. The United Nations Commission on International Trade Law (UNCITRAL) is currently working on a comprehensive reform of the investor-state dispute settlement (ISDS) system. The OECD is also embarked on a work programme on the Future of Investment Treaties, with one track addressing investment treaties and climate change, and the other considering updating older treaties to conform to approaches widely used in recent treaties.

Treaty innovations at regional and continental level in Africa

Different countries and regions have adopted different strategies for reform, and Africa has in many ways been at the forefront of innovative approaches. These can be seen in the non-binding Pan-African Investment Code, and likely in the Investment Protocol as part of the AfCFTA, once it is completed, as well as regional approaches in SADC, the Economic Community of West African States (ECOWAS) and elsewhere. They place much greater emphasis on achieving sustainable development outcomes from treaties, as explained below.

An increasing number of states and regional organisations, including African states and Regional Economic Communities, incorporate sustainable development considerations in their new investment agreements or model agreements and adopt innovative provisions on various policy issues. The analysis of some investment instruments adopted in Africa at the continental and regional levels reveals the states' desire to: (i) attract and protect investments that foster sustainable development; (ii) preserve their regulatory policy space, including on sustainable development-related policy issues, by better delineating and limiting some of the core standards of protection; (iii) achieve a better balance between the investors' and states' rights and obligations, including on sustainable development-related matters; (iv) make commitments on sustainable development-related issues; and (v) redesign the ISDS system.

This section reviews developments in the following regional and continental approaches:

- The SADC Protocol on Finance and Investment, particularly Annex 1 on co-operation on investment (SADC PFI, signed 2006, entered into force 2010 and as revised as per the Agreement Amending Annex 1 signed in 2017);
- The SADC Model BIT (2012, a 2017 version is not available);

- The ECOWAS Supplementary Act Adopting Community Rules on Investment and the Modalities for their Implementation (ECOWAS SA, signed 2008, in force 2009);
- The ECOWAS Common Investment Code (ECOWIC, adopted in 2018);
- The draft Pan-African Investment Code (PAIC, 2016).

Language in the Preamble and in separate articles

The preambles of the SADC Model BIT and the ECOWIC provide that the parties to these instruments are "seeking to promote, encourage and increase investment opportunities that enhance sustainable development within the territories of the State Parties". The preambles also often expressly recognise the key role of investment or the private sector in achieving various sustainable development objectives, such as the reduction of poverty, the increase of productive capacity or the furtherance of human rights and human development. All of the instruments repeat the sustainable development objective in a separate article. The SADC Model BIT, ECOWIC and PAIC set out the characteristics that an investment must have to be protected (based on the Salini test in the ICSID jurisprudence), including the "significant contribution to the host State's economic development" (e.g. art. 4(4) of the PAIC).

All instruments set out in their definition of "investment" several exclusions, particularly for "portfolio investments" and certain "investments of a speculative nature". This underlines the states' desire to attract long-term or more substantial investments which have a better chance to make a positive contribution to sustainable development. Some instruments, such as the ECOWIC and PAIC, also exclude from their coverage "investments in any sector sensitive to its development or which would have an adverse impact on its economy" (art. 1(h) and art. 4(4) respectively).

Better delineation of substantive standards of protection, affirmation of the state's right to regulate and general exclusions to seek to preserve policy space on key sustainable development-related matters

The investment instruments clarify, limit and sometimes delete certain substantive standards, mainly to preserve policy space. The most recent instruments all contain detailed provisions on non-discrimination (which usually cover the National Treatment (NT) and Most-Favoured Nation (MFN) principles, apart from the SADC instruments which only cover the former) and on the protection against expropriation. They set out numerous limitations and exceptions to these standards, some of which are particularly relevant from a sustainable development point of view. For instance, nearly all the instruments list examples of elements that should be considered when assessing whether investors or investments are in "like circumstances" for the purpose of NT or MFN principles and refer to the effect on the environment. Some also authorise the adoption of measures that derogate from the NT and/or MFN principles, including regulatory measures designed and applied to protect or enhance legitimate public welfare objectives, such as public health, safety and the environment (ECOWIC, art. 7; and PAIC, art. 8 and 10 – provided they are not arbitrary). Certain instruments also exclude from the scope of MFN treatment dispute settlement procedures and/or substantive obligations of other treaties (e.g. ECOWAS SA, art, 6(1) or PAIC, art. 7(4)) which preclude investors from invoking broader provisions than those contained in these instruments. Lastly, some instruments provide that measures designed and applied to protect or enhance legitimate public welfare objectives, such as public health, safety and the environment, do not constitute indirect expropriation (the PAIC adds that the measure must be non-discriminatory but not the revised version of Annex 1 of the SADC PFI, while the SADC Model BIT leaves a choice).

The most recent instruments do not include an FET provision. The initial version of Annex 1 to the ECOWAS SA contains the FET standard but qualifies it by reference to customary international law. Some instruments also list a series of obligations relating to procedural fairness which, if breached, could constitute a breach of this standard (ECOWAS SA, art. 19). The SADC Model BIT advocates for an alternative and more restrictive option, “fair administrative treatment”, which protects, inter alia, against denial of justice, un-remedied and egregious violations of due process, targeted discrimination on manifestly unjustified grounds and manifestly abusive treatment.

The instruments also aim at preserving the state’s right to regulate on sustainable development-related issues by affirming this right in the agreement and by providing general exceptions. All instruments except the ECOWAS ones refer to the right to regulate and/or to the balance of rights and obligations between investors and states in their preamble. The SADC instruments also contain a separate provision affirming, inter alia, the right to take regulatory or other measures to ensure that “development in their territory is consistent with the goals and principles of sustainable development, and with other legitimate social and economic policy objectives” (art. 20). All instruments except the Annex 1 of the SADC PFI (both versions) also set out general exceptions for various measures including, inter alia, those aimed at protecting human, animal or plant life and the environment or at promoting the achievement of equality in their territory or designed to protect or advance persons or categories of persons disadvantaged by long term historic discrimination (usually provided these are applied in a non-arbitrary and non-discriminatory manner). Certain instruments also authorise the state to take non-discriminatory measures to comply with its international obligations under other treaties, which could include, for instance, measures aimed at achieving the commitment of the Paris agreements or other conventions or standards that promote sustainable development (SADC Model BIT, art. 6, revised version of Annex 1 of the SADC PFI, art. 5).

Introduction of a broad range of investor obligations and mechanisms to address breaches

All instruments incorporate a broad range of obligations for investors, many of which relate to sustainable development (except for both versions of Annex 1 of the SADC PFI). The PAIC and the ECOWIC are the most comprehensive in this respect. All instruments set out a general obligation to comply with domestic laws and regulations for investors and/or their investments. Most (except both versions of Annex 1 of the SADC PFI) also incorporate more specific pre- and post-establishment obligations for investors on a wide range of topics, including the environment, labour practices and standards, human rights, corruption or corporate social responsibility (CSR).

Investors are required to conduct environmental and sometimes social impact assessment (ECOWAS SA, art. 12, ECOWIC, art. 27 and PAIC, art. 37) or to comply with the assessment screening criteria and processes applicable to the proposed investment, as required by the laws of the host state or home state or international standards, whichever is the most rigorous (SADC Model BIT, art. 13, which requires considering impacts on human rights). Many instruments specify that the precautionary principle should be applied when conducting such assessments and to decisions taken in relation to a proposed investment. Investors are also required to comply with domestic environmental laws and multilateral agreements (ECOWIC, art. 27), protect the environment in performing their activities (PAIC, art. 37), repair any damages caused (PAIC, art. 37; ECOWIC, art. 27), maintain an environmental management system (SADC Model BIT, art. 14) or use environmentally sound management practices (ECOWIC, art. 29).

All instruments (except both versions of Annex 1 of the SADC PFI) provide that investors shall not engage in corrupt practices (as a main author or as an accomplice) before or after the establishment of the investment. Many also impose obligations related to human rights (such as the obligation to uphold, support and respect such rights, not to undertake any act that would breach these rights or be an accomplice to such acts) and labour, such as the obligation to act in accordance with or apply the standards stipulated in the 1998 ILO Declaration (the SADC Model BIT and ECOWAS SA) or, more generally, to comply with international conventions on labour issues (the PAIC). Some instruments include specific obligations concerning CSR but also hortatory clauses. The ECOWIC provides that investors “shall endeavour to promote and engage in CSR in accordance with international best practices” (art. 34).

The ECOWIC and PAIC also include certain obligations but also hortatory clauses concerning the transfer and diffusion of technology (including horizontal obligations, i.e. applicable to the state as well). The ECOWIC imposes an obligation on investors “to adopt, where practicable in the course of their business activities, practices that permit the transfer and rapid diffusion of technologies” and “to diffuse technology and upgrades as well as improvements thereof through various mechanisms such as the demonstration and competition effects, the movement of labour from foreign affiliates to local firms and through the creation of linkages between foreign and local companies and their customers” (art. 47 and 48; the PAIC uses hortatory language for the first obligation).

The enforceability for such obligations can vary and is not always clear. The ECOWAS SA is the most comprehensive on this topic while both versions of Annex 1 of the SADC PFI and the ECOWIC remain silent. Various consequences are foreseen under different treaties. For instance, several instruments (i) provide that the tribunal or competent adjudicatory body shall consider whether an alleged breach of obligations raised by the host state, if proven, is materially relevant to the issues before it, and if so, what mitigating or off-setting effects this may have on the merits of a claim or on the damages awarded (if any); and (ii) authorise to bring counterclaims against the investor (SADC Model BIT, art. 19(1) and (2); ECOWAS SA, art. 18(2), (4) and (5) and PAIC, art. 43(1) and (2)). Some of these instruments authorise the home or host state (or other actors) to initiate proceedings before a tribunal established under the instrument or to initiate civil action before the domestic courts for the breach of certain or all obligations (ECOWAS SA, art. 18(3) and SADC Model BIT art. 19(3) and (4)).

The breaches of corruption-related obligations often have separate consequences. The ECOWAS SA provides that a breach of such obligations, if established by a court, can prevent an investor from initiating dispute settlement procedures under this instrument (art. 18(1)). The SADC Model BIT considers that a breach of the article on corruption is “deemed to constitute a breach of the domestic law of the Host State concerning the establishment and operation of an investment” and therefore constitutes a breach of the treaty (art. 10(3) and 17(4) respectively). Many instruments also require the state parties to prosecute, and where convicted, penalise such acts of corruption.

Lastly, certain instruments further provide that investors can be subject to civil actions before the domestic courts of their home state or the host state for acts and decisions made in relation to their investment when such acts and decisions have led to “significant damage, personal injuries or loss of life” in the host state (ECOWAS SA, art. 17; see also SADC Model BIT, art. 17 which also includes “omissions” and does not require that such acts, decisions or omissions are made in relation to investment). The SADC Model BIT further adds that “home states shall ensure that their legal systems and rules allow for, or do not prevent or unduly restrict such actions” (see also, ECOWAS SA, art. 29).

State commitments and obligations concerning key sustainable development matters

All instruments contain obligations and commitments for the state parties concerning key sustainable development matters, including on the environment, labour, human rights and corruption. Like for the investors' obligations, both versions of Annex 1 of the SADC PFI are relatively succinct on this issue. By contrast, the ECOWIC is particularly detailed and sets out a broad range of commitments and obligations for the member states.

All instruments explicitly require the state parties not to lower certain standards. Most provide that the states recognise that “it is inappropriate” to encourage investment by relaxing labour, health, safety or environmental measures or some subset of these measures (both versions of Annex 1 of the SADC PFI, art. 13 and 11, ECOWAS SA, art. 20) or “domestic environmental and labour legislation” (SADC Model BIT). The ECOWIC goes further by providing that member states recognise that “it is unlawful” “to encourage investment by relaxing national health, safety or environmental measures” and by “reducing the protection afforded in their respective environmental laws” (art 21-22). Concerning labour, the ECOWIC uses less stringent language and provides that member states recognise that “it is inappropriate to encourage investment by relaxing domestic labour legislation" (art. 30). As a consequence, states parties commit not to waive or derogate from these measures and laws as an encouragement for investment. The original and revised versions of Annex 1 of the SADC PFI add that member states "agree not to waive or other derogate from international treaties they have ratified" as an encouragement for investment (art. 13 and 11). It is worth noting that the SADC Model BIT and ECOWIC provide for a consultation mechanism in case a member state breaches this obligation (art. 22(2) and. 21(4) respectively).

Many instruments include declarations and commitments by the state parties concerning their environmental, labour and human rights rules and standards. In certain instruments, the states, for instance, recognise the importance of multilateral agreements to which they are a party (ECOWIC, art. 23 for environmental agreements) or commit to implement them (ECOWIC, art. 23). Concerning domestic laws and regulations, most instruments provide that state parties shall (or "shall strive to") ensure that they provide for high levels of environmental, labour and/or human rights protection (in some cases adding that international standards or treaties shall be taken into account (ECOWAS SA, art. 21(2)) and shall strive to continue to improve those laws and regulations. Certain instruments add that they shall also ensure their laws and regulation are consistent with international labour standards and/or international human rights agreements (ECOWAS SA, art. 21).

Many of the instruments also impose obligations on the states concerning the fight against corruption (ECOWIC, Chapter 9, SADC Model BIT, art. 10 and ECOWAS SA, art. 30). Noticeably, the ECOWIC contains an obligation to ratify or adhere to the UN Convention against Corruption (art. 35(4)). Certain instruments, particularly the PAIC but more importantly the ECOWIC, impose other obligations on the states e.g. concerning the protection of the environment. The PAIC provides that the states shall undertake environmental impact assessments and that, with the investors, they should take all practical steps to promote, facilitate and finance the transfer of or access to environmentally sound technology and know-how (art. 30 and 37). In the ECOWIC, the member states also recognise the importance of public participation and regional co-operation on this important issue (art. 26(1)).

The instruments include various other commitments and obligations for the states which could also affect sustainable development, concerning, for instance, investment promotion and facilitation (including through investment promotion agencies and through the home state's assistance), the transparency and accessibility of investment legal framework, the co-operation on investment related issues or the protection of fair competition or intellectual property rights.

Alternatives and additions to the traditional ISDS mechanism

Faced with growing criticism of the ISDS mechanism, the instruments adopt different innovative approaches: ISDS is either excluded or, if included, is subject to various conditions, such as prior consultations and negotiations, exhaustion of domestic remedies or respect of certain time limits. Many instruments also encourage the use of alternative dispute resolution mechanisms such as mediation before initiating arbitration proceedings. These modifications reduce the risk of potential challenges to non-discriminatory regulatory measures, such as those adopted to achieve sustainable development objectives.

The original version of Annex 1 of the SADC PFI contains an ISDS provision. Under this instrument, investor-state disputes which have not been amicably settled, can be submitted to arbitration but only after exhaustion of local remedies (art. 28). The SADC Model BIT's preferred option is a state-state dispute settlement mechanism, which allows the state parties to bring claims on behalf of the investor subject to the fulfilment of several conditions (exhaustion of local remedies and respect of certain time limits to bring the claim) (art. 28). It sets out an example of an ISDS provision, in case the states decide to negotiate and include such a mechanism in their agreement but sets out numerous conditions (including those mentioned above) (art. 29). The 2016 version of Annex 1 of the SADC PFI deleted the ISDS provision but guarantees investors access to the domestic courts "for redress of their grievance in relation to any matter concerning their investment" (art. 25).

The language used in the ECOWAS SA is not fully clear on whether investor-state arbitration is possible. The ECOWIC provides that disputes between an investor and a member state may be resolved through various means including arbitration. The latter may be conducted at "any established public or private alternative dispute resolution centres or the arbitration division of the ECOWAS Court of Justice" but encourages use of regional and local alternative dispute settlement institutions. The Code adds that when investment contracts between a member state and an investor provide for the use of international mechanisms such as ICSID or UNCITRAL, the parties to such contracts "shall exhaust all local remedies including the ECOWAS Court of Justice or national dispute settlement systems" before resorting to these mechanisms (art. 54).

Mbengue and Schacherer (2021[2]) (OECD, 2022[1]) argue that the PAIC "offers a middle ground solution to African States that are either pro-ISDS or anti-ISDS" as it leaves the use of ISDS to the discretion of member states. The PAIC provides that "member states may, in line with their domestic policies, agree to utilise the [ISDS] mechanism" (art. 42(1)). Disputing parties must first seek resolution through consultations and negotiations, if they fail, the dispute may be resolved through arbitration, subject to the applicable laws of the host state and/or the mutual agreement of the parties and subject to exhaustion of local remedies (art. 43(1(d)). The PAIC also contains a fork-in-the-road provision preventing multiple proceedings (art. 43(2)).

Investment laws of the SADC Member States

The introduction of innovative provisions at the regional and continental levels seems to have had some spill-over benefits at domestic regulatory level. While domestic investment laws have a wider scope than IIAs – covering, for instance, the regulation of the admission of investments or the provision of incentives – they may also contain similar features, such as rights and guarantees for investors and investments.

While investment legislation involves many layers of rules and regulations covering different areas, this analysis is limited only to investment laws (and, when easily identifiable, to the accompanying regulations). It does not cover, for instance, general tax laws which may offer additional incentives, nor enterprise laws or commercial codes acts which may impose separate obligations on investors, as well as arbitration laws. This analysis also does not cover sectoral legislation which may regulate investment in specific sectors, nor wider legislation and constitutions which may provide further details on, for instance, the rules for nationalisation and expropriation. Consequently, it is not because a specific element aimed at enhancing sustainable development is absent from the investment law, such as an investor's obligation to protect the environment, that it is not provided for in separate legislation. Investment laws nevertheless often encapsulate a government's overall approach to investment policy and to the potential role of investment in attaining sustainable development objectives.

All SADC member states except Botswana and Lesotho have some form of an investment law, which, in most cases, covers both domestic and foreign investments. A third of these laws were adopted in the 1990s and 2000s and the rest in the 2010s and 2020s. The most recent laws are in South Africa, Namibia, Mauritius, Comoros, Angola and Zimbabwe. The laws described in this section are listed below:

- Angola: *Private Investment Law* (2018 – the 2021 amendment not included in the analysis)
- Botswana: none
- Comoros: *Investment Code* (2020)
- Democratic Republic of Congo: *Law on the Investment Code* (2002)
- Eswatini: *Investment Promotion Act* (1998)
- Lesotho: none

- Madagascar: Law 2007-036 relating to Investment Law (2008)
- Malawi: *Investment and Exportation Promotion Act* (2012)
- Mauritius: *Economic Development Board Act* (2017, amended 2018, 2019, 2020)
- Mozambique: *Law on Investment* (1993); *Investment Regulations Decree* (2009)
- Namibia: *Investment Promotion Act* (2016, not yet in force);
- *Foreign Investment Act* (1990, amended 1993)
- Seychelles: *Investment Act* (2010); *Investment Regulations* SI 76 (2022)
- South Africa: *Protection of Investment Act* (2015)
- Tanzania: *Investment Act* (1997)
- Zambia: *Zambia Development Agency Act* (2006, amended 2021)
- Zimbabwe: *Zimbabwe Investment and Development Agency Act* (2020)

The length and scope of the investment laws vary from one country to another. Some laws, such as in Mauritius and Malawi, focus primarily on the trade and investment promotion agency and do not provide any rights or guarantees for investors. Others are more general and cover a wide range of topics, such as: the rights, guarantees and, in some instances, obligations of investors and investments; the conditions for market access; the different advantages and incentives and their eligibility conditions; the rules on investment in special economic zones; and the establishment and role of the trade and investment agency.

South Africa's 2015 law was adopted following the country's decision to terminate many of its BITs and aims to replace existing BITs. Its content is therefore relatively close to an IIA (i.e. it focuses on the investor's guarantees and on the state's rights and does not cover other topics such as incentives or conditions for market access). It is also important to note that, in 2016, Namibia adopted a new investment law which does not seem to be enforced yet. In 2021, the United States State Department noted that "the country ha(d) not yet enforced this Act due to substantive legal concerns raised by the private sector" concerns (for instance, it requires prior approval before investing in the country), and that the *Foreign Investment Act of 1990* "remain(ed) the guiding legislation on investment in Namibia" (US DoS, 2021[3]). Both laws have thus been reviewed for the purpose of this study.

The introduction of innovative provisions at the regional and continental level seems to have had some spill over benefits at domestic regulatory level. Some of the most recent laws reveal the states' desire to (i) attract and protect investments that could positively contribute to sustainable development; (ii) better delineate the scope of protection clauses in order to avoid any ambiguity and to reinforce the State's right to regulate on public policy issues; (iii) provide not only rights but also obligations for investors in investment laws, including on sustainable development related issues (albeit limited); and (iv) rethink the investor-state dispute mechanisms. In contrast with the regional/continental investment instruments analysed above, the SADC investment laws impose limited commitments and obligations on the state concerning sustainable development related issues.

Sustainable development is rarely a central objective of the investment laws but certain elements are taken into account when applying for investment approval or incentives

Unlike the SADC regional investment instruments, half of SADC members with an investment law make no reference to sustainable development either in a preamble or in related articles. Only three include a reference to sustainable development or some aspects in the preamble. Namibia's 2016 law states in its preamble that this Act "provide(s) for the promotion of sustainable economic development and growth through the mobilisation and attraction of foreign and domestic investment". The Act repeats this objective in a separate provision. The preamble of South Africa's 2015 law also recognises "the importance that investment plays in job creation, economic growth, sustainable development, and the well-being of the people of South Africa". The objectives of this Act focus on achieving a better balance between the rights and obligations of investors and states and at affirming the state's sovereign right to regulate investments in the public interest (see preamble and Section 4) – which, as explained above, could support sustainable development if the investors' obligations and the state's right to regulate were directed towards the achievement of sustainable development objectives. Angola's 2018 law lists the "goals regarding (the) granting of benefits and concessions", which include sustainable development related objectives such as stimulating the creation of new jobs for national workers, increasing the Angolan workforce's professional qualifications, promoting the transfer of knowledge and technology and increasing productive efficiency and competitiveness (art. 22). Zambia refers to economic growth and promotion and encouragement of education and skills training to increase productivity.

Other investment laws include a reference to sustainable investment in related articles. Mozambique's law provides that the investment covered by this law "should contribute to the sustainable economic and social development of the country" (art. 6). The law also lists a series of more precise objectives for investment, some of which relate to sustainable development objectives, notably concerning productivity and labour. Angola's 2018 law provides that private investment carried out according to this law "must contribute to economic and social development" (art. 3).

Other laws condition the granting of investment approval or incentives on certain sustainable development related elements. The DRC sets out various eligibility conditions to benefit from the general regime of incentives which include an undertaking to comply with legislation and regulations concerning the protection of the environment and to train local workers for technical and managerial positions (art. 8). The investment laws of Namibia (1993 and 2016), Zambia and Zimbabwe also list various sustainable development elements among the elements that the competent authority should take into account when considering an application for a licence, certificate for registration or approval of investment (to benefit from certain advantages or to be able to invest in a business or, more broadly, in the country). Namibia's 2016 law, for instance, provides that "(I)n considering the application for approval of investment [...], the minister must consider the net benefit for Namibia, taking into account" various elements, including "the contribution of the investment to the advancement of persons who have been socially, economically or educationally disadvantaged by past discriminatory laws and practices" or "to the transfer of technological and managerial skills, knowledge and innovation" and "the impact on the environment and contribution to environmental benefits" (sec. 14).

Better delineation of the investors' standards of protection in some more recent laws

Like the SADC investment instruments, some of the most recent investment laws tend to better delineate the standards of protection for investors and to set out limitations and exceptions to these standards, including, in some limited cases, to protect the states' right to regulate on sustainable development related matters. The analysis below focuses on the non-discrimination principle, the protection against expropriation and the FET standard.

Most investment laws have a separate provision on the principle of non-discrimination post-establishment, although some of the most recent ones contain more detailed provisions. Like many SADC investment instruments, Namibia, South Africa, and Zimbabwe's investment laws provide guidance on how to interpret 'like circumstances' with respect to NT or MFN treatment (and some of them list the same circumstances, i.e. the effect on third persons and the local community and on the environment). While several laws set out exceptions to these standards, a limited number directly relate to the state's right to regulate on key sustainable development matters. The most relevant examples of exclusions concern the benefit of any treatment, preference or privilege resulting from "any law or measure the purpose of which is to promote the achievement of equality in South Africa or designed to protect or advance persons or categories of persons, historically disadvantaged by unfair discrimination on the basis of race, gender or disability in the Republic" (South Africa, sec. 8), or the procedures for the resolution of investment disputes between foreign investors and the state provided for in international investment treaties and trade agreements (Zimbabwe, sec. 14).

All investment laws (except those of Malawi and Mauritius) contain a provision on the protection against expropriation, with the most recent laws often more precise on this standard than the older ones, including guidance on how to determine whether a specific measure or act constitutes an indirect expropriation (e.g. Comoros, art. 9), or on how to assess the compensation for expropriation (e.g. Namibia, 2016, sec. 22). Only Comoros and Zimbabwe set out express exceptions to this standard that would support the state's right to regulate on sustainable development matters. Like some SADC investment instruments, these laws provide that non-discriminatory measures designed and applied to protect legitimate public welfare objectives, such as public health, security and the environment do not constitute an indirect expropriation. Zimbabwe sets out a limit to this exception, i.e. "except in the rare circumstance when the impact of a measure or a series of measures is so severe in light of its purpose that it appears manifestly excessive" (sec. 17(7)).

The FET standard is rarely included in investment laws. Four SADC member states have decided to include this standard, or an alternative standard, in their investment laws. Seychelles (sec. 4) has opted for an unqualified FET, undertaking to provide FET, in accordance with the principles of international law, to investors and investments (art. 25). Zimbabwe defines this standard in a more precise way and lists the type of acts which could lead to a breach of FET (sec. 16). Lastly, South Africa's 2015 law contains an alternative standard proposed in the SADC Model BIT, i.e. the fair and administrative treatment (although its content is slightly different).

South Africa's law not only clarifies some of the substantive standards of protection but also provides guidance on how to interpret and apply the Act. Section 3 provides that the "Act must be interpreted and applied in a manner that is consistent with": (a) its purposes as contemplated by section 4; (b) the Constitution, including (i) the interpretation of the Bill of Rights, customary international law and international law as contemplated in various sections of the Constitution, and (c) any relevant convention or international agreement to which the Republic is or becomes a party. It is also the only SADC investment law to contain a separate provision reaffirming the state's right to regulate, including on issues such as the protection of the environment and the conservation and sustainable use of natural resources (sec. 12) (in contrast with the SADC instruments which all contain a separate provision).

Namibia's 2016 law is also the only one to contain a general exception provision, including for concessions, advantages, exemptions in favour of a foreign or domestic investor or investment that may result from any bilateral or multilateral treaty relating to investment or free trade or economic agreement to which it is a party (sec. 20).

Relatively limited sustainable development-related obligations for investors and investments and enforcement mechanisms

While most SADC investment instruments impose a broad range of sustainable development related obligations on investors and their investments, relatively few national investment laws do so (the original and revised versions of Annex 1 of the SADC PFI similarly contain few of these obligations). Noticeably, South Africa's law does not set out any obligations for investors, even though one of its purposes is to "protect investment in accordance with and subject to the Constitution, in a manner which balances the public interest and the rights and obligations of investors" (sec. 4).

Like in the SADC investment instruments, the most common feature found in the SADC investment laws is the inclusion of a general obligation for investors or their investment to comply with domestic legislation. Investment laws in Namibia (2016), Angola and Zimbabwe, for instance, contain a separate positive obligation for investors requiring them to "respect", "comply with" or "abide by" the domestic laws and regulations in force in their country.

A limited number of investment laws impose pre-establishment obligations. The most relevant example from a sustainable development perspective is Mozambique's law which requires investors to submit "the relevant studies and evaluations of the environmental impact and of any pollution and sanitation concerns that may result from their activities, and the damages and/or wastes of their undertakings" (Article 26). Zimbabwe's law contains a more limited obligation concerning public-private partnership projects, requiring a feasibility study for these projects, which shall, inter alia, demonstrate that the project will "not adversely impact the environment or mitigate or address any such adverse impacts" (4 Schedule, Part II, sec, 4(2)(c)). Several laws also sanction the provision of false or misleading statements, in various aspects, including when applying for a licence, permit or certificate in relation to the investment, which could be interpreted as a "pre-establishment obligation". While such an obligation does not directly relate to key sustainable development related matters, it could help governments to fully understand and assess the potential impact of a proposed investment projects on sustainable development.

The investment laws more frequently impose post-establishment obligations which either apply to all investors or only to those benefiting from specific advantages or incentives. While some of these obligations concern sustainable development related matters, they are more limited in scope and content than those contained in the investment instruments analysed above.

Some of the oldest laws were quite advanced on this topic and impose obligations in relation to the protection of the environment or to labour. Mozambique requires investors and their companies to undertake "appropriate measures for the prevention and minimisation of any negative environmental effects" and provides that activities "with levels of pollution and contamination likely to alter and negatively affect the environment or public health shall comply with restrictions established by law and/or issued by competent authorities, as well as any rules or international agreements on such issues" to which the country is a signatory (art. 26). DRC imposes various obligations on companies that benefit from incentive regimes including in relation to the environment (obligation to comply with the regulations on the environment and conservation of biodiversity) and labour standards and practices (compliance with labour legislation and provision of professional training) (art. 31).

The most recent laws set out various post-establishment obligations, including in relation to sustainable development. Namibia's 2016 law incorporates several investor obligations in relation to labour standards. For instance, it requires investors to "absorb available skills in the Namibian labour market", to "invest in human capacity in the Namibian labour market" and "ensure the transfer of skills to the Namibian" "so as to enhance the sustainability of the investment and its linkage with the Namibian economy and achieving the developmental objectives of Namibia" (sec. 24). Angola's law has a separate provision setting out the "specific duties" of private investors, which include obligations related to the environment (respecting the norms regarding the defence of the environment) and labour standards (respecting the norms regarding hygiene, protection and safety at work against occupational diseases or work accidents contained in the labour legislation) (art. 18). It also contains an article which imposes obligations concerning the employment and training of local workers (art. 46). Comoros sets out various obligations for investors and enterprises which benefit from an incentive regime concerning labour practices (priority employment of local workers when equal qualification, providing them training and developing their skills) (art. 17). Lastly, Zimbabwe's law contains a separate article on the "responsibility of investors" which set out "common obligations", including the obligation to preserve the environment (art. 21).

The enforceability for such obligations can vary and is not always clear. SADC investment instruments contain a broad range of mechanisms to sanction the potential breach of investor obligations, but this approach has generally not yet been incorporated in national investment laws. Most of these laws address the consequences of the provision of false or misleading information mainly in connection with an application for a licence or certificate. Such conduct can lead to the suspension or revocation of the licence and certificate and, in the most serious cases, to fines and imprisonment. A limited number of laws provide that the same sanctions may apply for other breaches, such as the "lack of execution of training actions" (Angola, art. 47), the company's failure to comply with its commitments or if it breaches legal provisions (DRC, art. 34) or more broadly, the breach of any domestic laws (Mauritius, sec. 14).

Limited sustainable development related obligations and commitments for states

Unlike in SADC investment instruments, national investment laws barely contain any states' obligations or commitments on key sustainable development issues such as the protection of the environment, the respect of labour standards and human rights, or the fight against corruption. None contain a provision precluding the state from lowering environmental, labour or other standards. Eswatini has the only law to contain an obligation concerning the fight against corruption (art. 23). Mozambique includes a very specific obligation concerning the protection of the environment (art. 23 requires the competent authorities to undertake an environmental impact assessment for special economic zones). Lastly South Africa's law sets out obligations and commitments concerning the fight against discrimination and the protection of human rights in its preamble.

Several SADC member states do however make other commitments in these laws which could positively contribute to sustainable development. For instance, certain members undertake to improve the transparency of the investment framework (Seychelles, sec. 7; Zimbabwe, sec. 18; and South Africa, preamble), or to protect intellectual property rights (see, Madagascar, art. 4 and Angola, art. 16). Most of these laws also contain provisions on the establishment and role of a specialised agency, whose main function is to promote and facilitate investment, which thus reinforces the possibility of attracting investment that could positively contribute to sustainable development.

Alternative and innovative approaches concerning ISDS in the most recent laws

Most of the older investment laws authorise recourse to arbitration for disputes between foreign investors (and sometimes domestic ones) and the state subject to relatively classic conditions, such as preliminary attempts at settling the dispute amicably (see e.g. Mozambique, sec. 25; Eswatini, art. 21; Tanzania, sec. 23; or DRC, Titre XI). In contrast, some of the most recent laws adopt new approaches concerning the resolution of such disputes, which reflect, to some extent, the approaches adopted in the SADC investment instruments, including the most recent ones. South Africa has decided to exclude ISDS completely, setting out various dispute resolution options for foreign investors, including recourse to mediation, to domestic courts or independent tribunals and to state-state arbitration but only with consent of the government and after exhaustion of domestic remedies (sec. 13).

Other recent laws provide for ISDS but incorporate various limitations in its use. Namibia's 2016 law provides that foreign investors may request the minister responsible for investment to designate a mediator or mediation panel to resolve the dispute but authorises them to directly approach the domestic courts instead of using mediation. It further provides that the jurisdiction over disputes relating to this Act "lies exclusively with the courts of Namibia" but authorises to submit such disputes to arbitration under the *Arbitration Act* of 1965, subject to written agreement between the minister and the investor or investment (sec. 28). Zimbabwe authorises investors to resort to (i) domestic arbitration in accordance with the *Arbitration Act 1996* or (ii) any other international arbitration referred by mutual agreement of the parties. It also authorises foreign investors to submit the dispute to the mechanisms set out in the IIAs signed between Zimbabwe and their home state. The Act however requires them to register their investment with the Investment and Development Agency within specific time limits. Failing this, they "shall be deemed to have waived the protection" of these agreements, "with the result that any dispute in relation thereto can only be settled by a domestic court or domestic arbitration" (sec. 38).

In contrast, Comoros's law authorises domestic and foreign investors to resort to ISDS (with different arbitration rules) with relatively few limitations (parties can also agree to submit the dispute to domestic courts but subject to the fork-in-the road provision) (art. 12). Angola's law is very succinct on this point; it guarantees the investors' access to the domestic courts but also provides that conflicts that may eventually arise regarding available rights might be resolved through alternative methods of resolving conflicts, namely negotiation, mediation, conciliation and arbitration, as long as that by special law there are not subjected to judicial court or necessary arbitration (art. 15).

Table 2.1 compares the provisions at the regional level with those of national investment laws in SADC member states as they relate to sustainable development. This summary of provisions in a binary fashion does not do full justice to the possible qualifications that might be included in any given provision, but overall it does provide a quick overview of the extent to which national investment laws fully reflect the innovations at regional level and which are most likely to be found in the forthcoming AfCFTA Investment Protocol. The regional and country-level approaches are described in more detail below.

Table 2.1. National investment laws in SADC do not fully reflect broader regional approaches

	SADC Model BIT	SADC IPF 2016	National investment laws
References to sustainable development, state's right to regulate or investor obligations in preamble or other general provisions	Yes	Yes	Yes = 7 No = 8
Limitations on the protection against expropriation (e.g. public health, security and the environment)	Yes	Yes	Yes = 2 No = 13
National treatment	Yes	Yes	Yes = 11 No = 4
Limitations on NT, e.g. when assessing "like circumstances"	Yes	Yes	Yes = 9 No = 2
Fair and equitable treatment (FET)	Either yes but qualified by customary international law or Fair Administrative Treatment	No	Yes (qualified) = 1 Yes (unqualified) = 1 No = 13
General exceptions for measures relating to sustainable development	Yes	No, except compliance with other treaties	
Compliance with domestic laws	Yes	Yes	Yes = 9 No = 6
Pre-establishment obligations (environment, labour, human rights, CSR, corruption)	Yes	No	Yes = 5 No = 10
Post-establishment obligations (environment, labour, human rights, CSR, corruption)	Yes	No	Yes = 12 No = 3

Source: OECD compilation

References

African Union (2019), *African Continental Free Trade Area Agreement*, https://au-afcfta.org/afcfta-legal-texts/. [4]

Mbengue, M. and S. Schacherer (2021), "Evolution of International Investment Agreements in Africa: Features and Challenges of Investment Law "Africanization"", in *Handbook of International Investment Law and Policy*, Springer Singapore, Singapore, https://doi.org/10.1007/978-981-13-5744-2_77-2. [2]

OECD (2022), *FDI Qualities Policy Toolkit*, OECD Publishing, Paris, https://doi.org/10.1787/7ba74100-en. [1]

SADC (2018), *SADC Model BIT*, http://www.sadc.int/. [5]

SADC (2016), *SADC Investment Policy Framework*, https://www.sadc.int/pillars/investment. [6]

US DoS (2021), *2021 Investment Climate Statements: Namibia*, https://www.state.gov/reports/2021-investment-climate-statements/namibia/. [3]

3 Promoting sustainable investment

This chapter provides an overview of investment promotion agencies (IPAs) in SADC Member States and on their main priorities and efforts to attract sustainable investment. It also draws on the experience of other regions to provide lessons on better targeting FDI to support sustainable development and sharpening the indicators used for this purpose.

Governments prepare investment promotion strategies to support the achievement of national development objectives through the promotion and facilitation of foreign direct investment (FDI). As these strategies are designed to influence the kind of investments that are attracted, governments focus on certain types of investments over others by selecting priority sectors, countries and investors (OECD, 2018[1]). This prioritisation takes place because some types of FDI, with certain characteristics, are considered to make more of a contribution to a host country's development than other types (Sauvant and Mann, 2017[2]). In particular, the issues of sustainability, inclusiveness and the contribution to the sustainable development goals (SDGs) have become increasingly important and have led some agencies to redefine their priorities. This chapter provides an overview of investment promotion agencies (IPAs) in SADC Member States and on their main priorities and efforts to attract sustainable investment. It also draws on the experience of other regions to provide lessons on better targeting FDI to support sustainable development and sharpening the indicators used for this purpose.

Promoting and facilitating investment in SADC

The role of national investment promotion agencies

IPAs are the key point of contact between the government and investors, providing tailored services that aim at ensuring a simplified, clear and engaging experience for private sector stakeholders to do business within the country. IPAs also implement national investment promotion strategies by attracting firms in priority sectors with potential for growth and spillovers (OECD, 2018[1]). In the SADC region, all Member States have well-established IPAs, dating back to the Lesotho National Development Corporation founded in 1967 (later reformed to consolidate investment promotion and facilitation functions in 1990 and 2000) until the establishment of the Zimbabwe Investment Development Corporation in 2020. Half of SADC Member States' IPAs were originally established as individual agencies while the other half were born from mergers of several bodies responsible for investment, trade and commerce to create dedicated authorities on tailored investment promotion, facilitation and retention services.

Experienced and inclusive governance of IPAs, typically exerted by a Board of Directors, can help ensure transparency, accountability and efficiency in carrying out their mandates (OECD, 2021[3]). Despite differences in institutional arrangements, all SADC IPAs comprise of Boards with the objective to oversee and approve the activities of the agency. The composition of directors, as mandated by their respective legislations, requires the inclusion of both private and public sector representatives in the Democratic Republic of the Congo (DRC), Eswatini, Lesotho, Madagascar, Mauritius, Namibia, Seychelles, Tanzania, Zambia, and Zimbabwe. Including private sector actors ensures that the interests of businesses are considered which can play a role in streamlining administrative processes and procedures. However, the inclusion of other institutions such as research, academia and civil society actors is not mandatory for all countries, with the exception of Zambia which requires the inclusion of sector-specific representatives and civil society organisations. Most others have positions that may be filled based on specified qualifications concerning characteristics such as ownership stake and corporate management experience at the discretion of the chairman or director. Some IPAs include additional supervisory roles in addition to the Board of Directors to oversee specific functions more extensively, such as audit or technical committees that focus on financial and accounting issues.

Investment generation efforts are at the centre of IPAs' role in attracting investors and using FDI to advance national economic and strategic goals. Operating regional and foreign branches can help spread awareness about location-specific advantages and instil greater investor confidence. International branches have the added benefit of proximity to potential investor targets and can execute proactive approaches to engage with local companies (Knoerich and Vitting, 2021[4]). Branch offices remain uncommon for IPAs in SADC, with only a handful of countries, including Botswana, Comoros, Malawi, South Africa and Tanzania are holding regional offices. Botswana also operates foreign branches in India, the United Kingdom and South Africa, while Mauritius operates eight units that manage investment promotion efforts in France, South Africa, India, Japan, Kenya, Singapore, China and the United Arab Emirates (UAE), the only countries in the region to manage international offices outside of embassy and consular functions.

All SADC IPAs operate one-stop shops that facilitate the incorporation of businesses, helping them navigate sometimes cumbersome and complex regulatory systems. In addition to clerical assistance for obtaining permits, business licenses, tax and other business procedures to start or expand operations, the IPAs' one-stop-shops provide information on the legal framework for investment, investment opportunities, incentives and grants. Twelve of the region's 16 agencies also provide investors with adapted strategic advice while ten agencies advocate for investor needs with policy makers (Figure 3.1). Less common are business to business matchmaking events and forums that promote partnerships and local linkages for value chain integration offered by eight agencies, and monitoring of ongoing investment projects offered by only six countries.

Figure 3.1. Main services provided by SADC IPAs

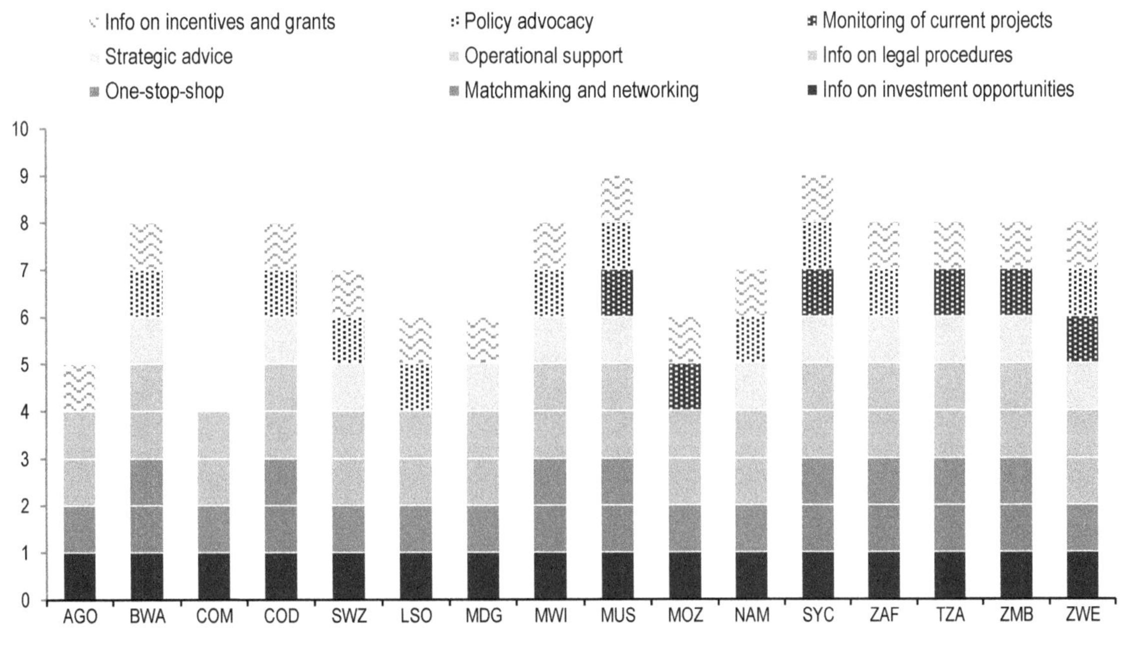

Source: OECD compilation based on IPAs' websites [accessed in March 2023].

Digitalisation of IPA services

While some IPAs continue to carry out services physically through in-person offices, many amenities provided by SADC IPAs have been digitalised through online one-stop-shop services for administrative registrations and procedures. While the mobility restrictions caused by the COVID-19 pandemic prompted IPAs to change their priority actions and ways of working (OECD, 2020[5]), several SADC IPAs further expanded their e-services much like the IPAs of OECD countries. The IPAs of Mauritius, Botswana and Zambia moved substantial parts of their investment promotion activities online, participating in virtual trade exhibitions and seminars to facilitate engagement between investors and businesses while promoting local manufacturers in place of traditional business forums and business to business meetings. During 2020, the Zambian Development Agency implemented a total of 14 virtual inward and outward investment-oriented missions with international partners as well as 4 virtual local business to business forums while continuing to conduct 130 industrial visits throughout the year. IPAs with offices abroad remained active through participation in online conferences, dissemination of promotional material and virtual outreach meetings with potential investors. The international offices of Mauritius' Economic Development Board (EDB) organised and took part in several webinars with foreign partners in Africa and Asia to support the ratification of free trade agreements while the international offices of Botswana's BITC used various digital platforms to conduct virtual outward missions with potential investors from South Africa, Poland, Germany and India.

Although the use of digital one-stop-shops and online business services promotes wider coverage and simplified administrative procedures, it also raises additional issues connected to the condition of the overall digital ecosystem and access to such services for less electronically linked communities. One-stop-shop services also depend on the reliability of systems related to data submission, data exchange, electronic signature systems, information sharing, and potential delegation of responsibility.

Promoting investment at the regional level

SADC Member States have sought to integrate investment policies to better serve regional development efforts since 2006 through the adoption of the SADC Protocol on Finance and Investment.[1] The Protocol emphasises the importance of regional co-operation in the area of investment promotion and facilitation to ensure economic and social development of the region as a whole (SADC, 2006[6]). It specifically encourages Member States' IPAs to:

- carry out their national investment promotion activities in line with regional development priorities;
- advise and include neighbouring governments, the private sector and other stakeholders in the formulation and review of policies and procedures that affect investment and trade; and
- increase awareness of national investment incentives, opportunities, legislation, practices, major events affecting investments and other relevant activities with regional peers through regular exchange of information.

Priority sectors and sustainability in SADC

SADC prioritise the promotion of key sectors for investment based on factors such as the profitability of projects in certain industries, socio-economic growth models and alignment with national development plans. The agriculture and tourism and hospitality sectors are the most frequently promoted sectors, prioritised by every IPA in the region, followed by energy, manufacturing and technology and communication services (Table 3.1). While the objectives of promoting tourism are diverse, the prioritisation of the agriculture industry in SADC is exclusively aimed at ensuring food security and increasing the self-sufficiency of food production, including the development of relevant infrastructure and facilities. While the IPAs from Mauritius and South Africa promote the largest array of sectors on their websites or within their strategies, those from Mozambique and Zambia are the most selective agencies.

Table 3.1. Main sectors promoted by SADC IPAs

	AGO	BWA	COM	COD	SWZ	LSO	MDG	MWI	MUS	MOZ*	NAM	SYC	ZAF	TZA	ZMB	ZWE
Agriculture / forestry																
Construction / infrastructure																
Education*																
Energy																
Incl. renewable energy																
Finance / insurance																
Fishing / Blue economy																
Health																
Manufacturing																
Mining																
Technology / Communication																
Tourism / hospitality																
Transportation / logistics																

Note: Information on Mozambique may not be up-to-date due to website inaccessibility.
Source: OECD compilation based on IPAs' websites.

Capitalising on renewable energy opportunities

SADC agencies are moving focus towards investment in sustainable development, with almost two-thirds of their IPAs promoting specific opportunities for renewable energy projects either in their investment promotion or national development strategies, or directly on their IPA websites. Some agencies have achieved a further level of drawing attention to sustainable investment opportunities in their countries. Tanzania recently launched the SDG Investments Tanzania Platform that provides specific data and insights on indicative returns, investment and market timeframes, range of required investment amounts and regional prospects for SDG-aligned investment opportunities. Some countries have also moved towards promoting investment in niche clean energy sectors. Namibia's IPA is focusing efforts on maximising investment in projects concerning green hydrogen and green ammonia production to pursue its long-term goal of climate neutrality under the Harambee Prosperity Plan II (2021 – 2025), going as far as the establishment of an additional Inter-Ministerial Green Hydrogen Council in 2021.

IPAs can also assist investors by streamlining the information and regulatory process for environmentally and socially sustainable projects. For example, the IPAs of Lesotho, Madagascar, Namibia, Tanzania and Zambia provide feasibility studies for potential sites of activity based not only on financing considerations, but also on variables such as adequate existing natural resources and rural settlement patterns. Madagascar's IPA has streamlined and simplified its authorisation and concession schemes for renewable energy investments and reformulated its planning and pricing principles related to these projects in line with the green objectives of the New Energy Policy (2015) and New Electricity Code (2017).

In an effort to avoid, minimise and mitigate any negative ecological outcomes of large-scale projects, the majority of SADC regulatory frameworks also require the submission of environmental impact assessment (see chapter on Green Investment), the process of which can be supported by IPAs. As part of its promotion and facilitation services, the Lesotho National Development Corporation assists new investors in the preparation of project briefs necessary for environment impact assessments. Co-ordination of IPAs with other key ministries that handle sustainability-related sectors is also crucial in providing a coherent approach to ensuring investors meet sound environmental standards. Mozambique's AIPEX is responsible for smooth co-ordination with the Ministry of Environment to swiftly enable the issuance of environmental licenses to those projects that do not violate maximum effluent emission limits.

IPAs can also connect sustainability priorities when it comes to renewable initiatives, promoting integration of domestic value chains and upskilling opportunities for domestic labour forces. Invest South Africa (InvestSA) leverages FDI in renewable power generation to promote domestic manufacturing of equipment used for renewable energy projects. It does this by initiating effective consultations with other government agencies to develop an understanding of the potential for localisation through inter-institutional feasibility studies and continuous collaboration with relevant ministries on technical matters, leaving the IPA with reliable information to demonstrate the benefits and practicality of localisation to potential investors. IPAs can also help upskill the country's labour force to incentivise foreign investors to employ domestic workers with specific knowledge or training needed for the relevant industries. Zambia's ZDA offers several training programmes for entrepreneurs looking to open or expand businesses in the country, as well as agriculture business trainings and corporate governance trainings. IPAs can also encourage the upskilling of the domestic labour force by foreign investors through incentives, as is the case in Botswana whereby education and training grants are provided for investors to invest in the domestic workforce.

Promoting the preservation of the region's environment

Given the significant economic contribution of the ocean sectors and the impact climate change has on island nations, the IPAs of Comoros, Mauritius and the Seychelles have geared a large part of their environmental efforts to marine and blue economy. These represent various opportunities for investment, in addition to renewable energy solutions, in sectors such as fishing, coastal tourism, aquaculture, maritime services and waste management. The three agencies play an essential role in promoting the ocean economy, managing dedicated webpages that provide resources on and promote concrete blue investment opportunities. The EDB of Mauritius has a dedicated team responsible for well-established as well as emerging maritime activities to ensure sustainable use of ocean resources. The Seychelles Investment Board works closely with the Department of Blue economy to ensure that all investment and business activities within the ocean territories, including sustainable fisheries, eco-tourism, port development and renewable energy, are in line with the sustainable use of marine sources outlined in the Seychelles Marine Spatial Plan and the Blue Economy Strategic Framework and Roadmap (2018-30).

SADC puts a strong emphasis on investment promotion in the agriculture sector at a regional level, stressing the importance of promoting sustainable management of the environment and natural resources and highlighting opportunities at both the national and regional level for agricultural and non-agricultural value chain development. The SADC Secretariat works with national IPAs to encourage private sector and international investment in agricultural value chains by providing essential information and showcasing Member States' opportunities. At the national level, all IPAs promote the agricultural sector as a strategic priority for investment, showcasing specific opportunities that bring innovation, sustainability and growth in agribusiness. Lesotho's IPA, in co-operation with the Lesotho Diaspora Investment Group, launched a fresh produce trading platform for local farmers to enable greater access to markets and finance, allowing them to transition for subsistence to commercial farming. In addition to sectors with high potential for industrial development, InvestDRC actively promotes agricultural sectors of socio-economic importance for grassroots communities while Madagascar's EDBM is promoting opportunities to better the quality of several growing produce sectors and reduce harmful horticultural practices, particularly for palm oil extraction.

A focus on entering novel agricultural markets is also emerging in the region, as several IPAs begin to launch the promotion of agriculture opportunities in cannabis production. Hemp is an eco-friendly plant that uses a fraction of the water needed to grow cotton, absorbs more carbon dioxide per hectare than other crops and most trees, and can be used for numerous renewable products including food products, paper, biofuels, textiles and even building materials. The crop also has significant potential as a sustainable source for natural health industries as every part of the plant can be used for various medical, industrial and nutritional uses (UNCTAD, 2022[7]). Malawi, South Africa and Zimbabwe have been active in legalising and promoting large-scale farming of cannabis plants for medicinal use. Malawi passed the Cannabis Regulation Act in 2020, legalising the cultivation and processing of medicinal cannabis and industrial hemp, and subsequently inaugurated the Cannabis Regulatory Authority which co-ordinates closely with the MITC on licensing and one-stop-shop registration services. The MITC is actively promoting the sector, focusing on the opportunity the industry presents to open numerous domestic value chains and employment opportunities due to the wide variety of products can be produced from industrial and medicinal cannabis such as sustainable foods, textiles, paper, building materials, biofuels, plastic composites, pharmaceutical products. Zimbabwe's ZIDA facilitates investments into medicinal cannabis cultivation, processing and value addition, which are considered special investments under the Investment Stability Agreement, allowing them to benefit from an array of monetary and fiscal incentives. ZIDA not only plays a co-ordination role between the ministries of health, security, finance and agriculture to ensure smooth licensing and registration procedures through its one-stop-shop, but also raises industry awareness, promotes smaller out-growers and encourages localisation of investment value chains in the cannabis sector.

Forestry services are being further promoted by IPAs in SADC to not only manage and meet the needs of forest resources, but to rebuild environments already damaged by harmful practices in the industry. The IPA of the DRC promotes specific investment opportunities to restore lost forests and combat climate change, with ambitious project goals such as planting approximately 3 million hectares of forest by 2025 under afforestation and reforestation programmes. Malawi's MITC is promoting projects for forest management, replanting Pine and Eucalyptus Trees for controlled and sustainable wood processing with the aim of developing a workforce with forest management skills while contributing to the country's zero-carbon target and climate change mitigation goals. InvestSA offers several opportunities for sustainable investment in forestry including re-afforestation and new afforestation, bio-refinery and transformative technologies and R&D for packaging design and development. It also focuses on supporting skills development in agriculture and forestry sectors through partnerships with national universities, research institutions and the Department of Environment, Forestry and Fisheries.

IPA commitment to social initiatives and inclusive projects

Botswana' BITC identifies opportunities and initiatives that address issues such as gender-based violence, Inspiring the Girl Child and renovating the Monarch Destitute Centre in Francistown through its corporate social responsibility programme. Mauritius' EDB provides training to women-led businesses, coaching those owning or considering opening businesses in marketing strategies through international trade fairs as well as market-related soft skills trainings in communication and buyer negotiation. Madagascar promotes opportunities in sustainable sectors that typically employ women, for example, in the fashion business like raffia where women-run businesses and production facilities corner a majority of the world's market.

InvestSA is refocusing the strategic orientation of part of its aftercare services to include supporting multinational enterprises in facilitating the participation of disadvantaged populations based on race, gender, disability and rural communities while prioritising re-investments with strong possibilities for sustainable impact. The agency has been active in facilitating partnerships between foreign enterprises and local marginalised communities. InvestSA has also begun to integrate gender-related indicators into their client relations management systems to be able to include them when evaluating investment leads. Zambia's ZDA monitoring and evaluation impact assessments of enterprises assess their developmental impact and contribution to corporate social responsibility. Similarly to InvestSA and ZDA, SADC IPAs would be well inspired to use their aftercare services to better promote responsible business conduct amongst the existing business community and encourage investors to comply with sustainability-related laws more systematically, as well as to embrace responsible practices in their business operations (see chapter on Responsible Business Conduct).

Promoting sustainable investment: experience from other regions

How IPAs can use FDI to support the SDGs

When governments design investment promotion strategies, they prioritise certain sectors, countries or investors, either because they have a higher probability of being realised or because they may bring certain benefits to the host economy (OECD, 2018[1]). Prioritisation strategies can be motivated by a series of different factors, depending mostly on the country's national development objectives, local assets and international context. These strategies allow countries to specialise and target their FDI attraction efforts towards specific government priorities.

As SADC IPAs recognise their role in attracting and boosting investment in support of the SDGs, benchmarking their efforts against those from other regions can allow them to make their investment promotion strategies more effective and to better prioritise investors that are more likely to generate sustainable development impacts. Findings from the *OECD survey on IPA Monitoring & Evaluation and Prioritisation*, covering member countries from the OECD and the Association of Southeast Asian Nations (ASEAN) show the importance that the SDGs can play – to varying degrees – in these countries' investment promotion strategies.

When asked about top factors influencing their investment promotion priorities, 56% of ASEAN IPAs have selected contributing to the SDGs, the highest share together with the political/ national agenda and digital transformation (Figure 3.2). This share is higher than in the OECD (44%), where agencies adopt a rather pragmatic approach and select the results of previous monitoring and evaluation (M&E) as the most important factor. The overall political or national agenda, which is also deemed important in both ASEAN and OECD countries, can underpin other factors as well, such as digitalisation and sustainability (OECD, 2023[8]). Conversely, the COVID-19 crisis is considered as a top factor by much fewer agencies. Although the pandemic has had a strong immediate effect on FDI flows and investment promotion activities around the world, it has not shifted their main concerns beyond key priorities such as sustainability and digitalisation. It has rather prompted governments and IPAs to accelerate their response to these global imperatives as a way to reinforce economic resilience.

As IPAs are increasingly targeting sustainable investment, they can contribute to some SDGs more than others. In both ASEAN and OECD countries, the SDGs relating to promoting economic growth and employment (Goal 8); ensuring access to modern and clean energy (Goal 7); and supporting resilient infrastructure, industrialisation and innovation (Goal 9) are mentioned by most IPAs (Figure 3.3). This is not a surprising result since these objectives correspond most closely to IPAs' usual tasks. ASEAN IPAs also consider contributing to a large extent to sustainability-related goals, particularly good health and well-being, sustainable cities and communities and life on land, while climate action is selected by 56% of ASEAN agencies and 37% of OECD.

Figure 3.2. Top factors motivating IPAs' current priorities in ASEAN and OECD countries

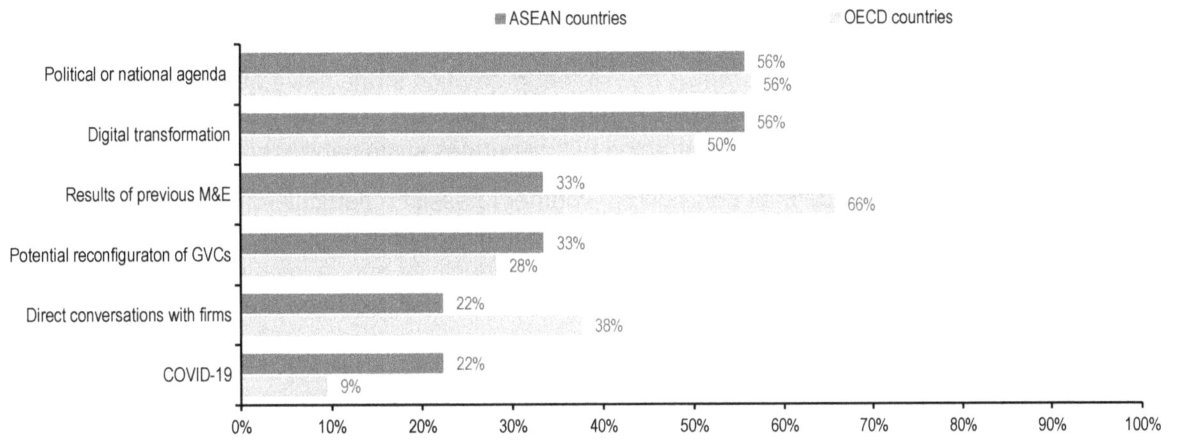

Source: OECD survey on IPA Monitoring & Evaluation and Prioritisation (OECD countries, 2021; ASEAN countries, 2022).

Figure 3.3. The SDGs to which IPAs in ASEAN and OECD contribute

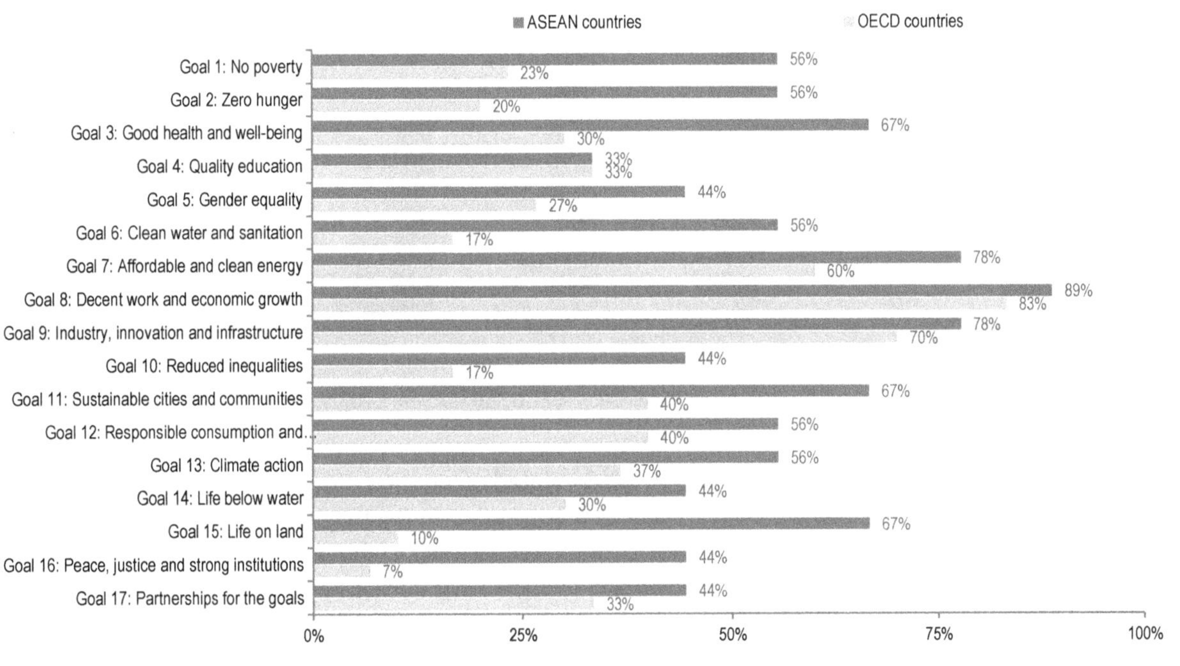

Source: OECD survey on IPA Monitoring & Evaluation and Prioritisation (OECD countries, 2021; ASEAN countries, 2022).

This reflects that ASEAN IPAs seem to contribute more to the SDGs than those in the OECD, which could be explained by the fact that IPAs in ASEAN are more often integrated in the ministry in charge of investment or have a broader economic role, which can thus give them a wider field of action on key aspects related to the SDGs (OECD, 2023[8]). IPAs in the OECD are often more specialised and autonomous, focusing on selected tasks and priorities, which are hence related to fewer SDGs. IPAs in SADC tend to have a more similar profile to OECD rather than ASEAN agencies and could have therefore similar trends.

Indicators to prioritise and measure the sustainability outcomes of FDI

A key question is the way and the degree to which IPAs can track their contribution to the SDGs, beyond the actual sectors they target. A closer look at their key performance indicators (KPIs) is necessary to understand and evaluate the extent to which investment promotion strategies contribute to attracting and facilitating sustainable investment. IPAs need to rely on specific and consistent indicators to ensure that they attract the right investments and the attracted FDI generates sustainability outcomes.

To select priority firms and guide their decision on whether to assist a particular investment project, IPAs rely on KPIs related to outcomes, which can be grouped into several categories. The most used KPIs in both ASEAN and OECD countries are those relating to productivity and innovation, and on job quantity and quality (Figure 3.4). This is likely to be the case in SADC as well, as these are the prime objectives of IPAs.

Figure 3.4. Types of KPIs used for FDI prioritisation by ASEAN and OECD agencies

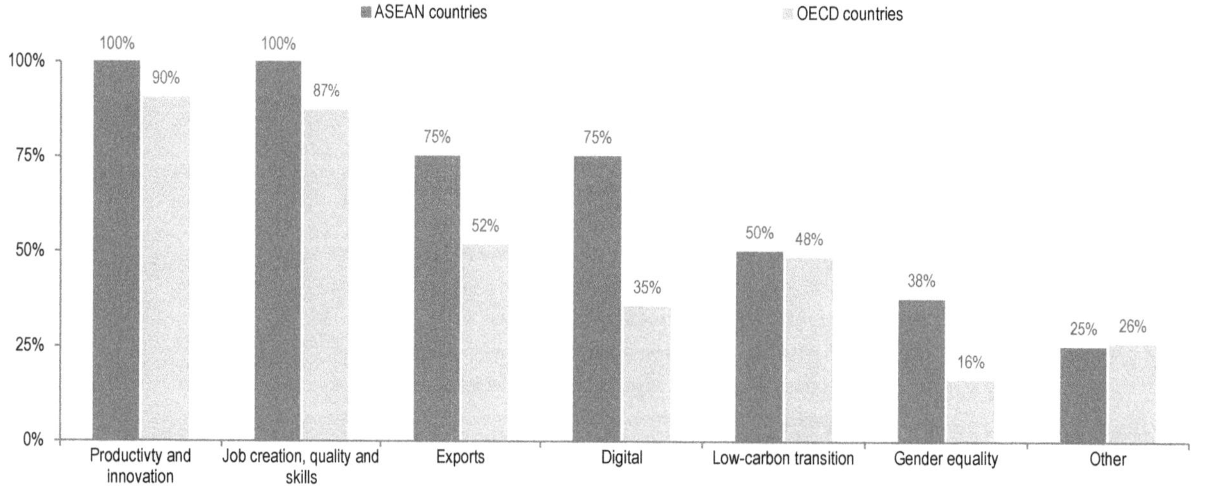

Source: OECD survey on IPA Monitoring & Evaluation and Prioritisation (OECD, 2021; ASEAN, 2022).

IPAs can also use KPIs that are related to other SDG-related categories. For example, the Philippines use indicators to prioritise investment projects that have a positive impact on nature conservation and the protection of sea and coastline. Indonesia uses an indicator relating to the geographical dispersion of FDI which measures the value of investment realisations outside Java (OECD, 2023[8]). Promoting investment in support of regional development has also become a high priority in OECD countries. As 92% of agencies have the mandate to promote and facilitate FDI in support of regional development, 69% use FDI distribution across regions as a KPI (OECD, 2022[9]).

KPIs related to the low-carbon transition are used by approximately half of the agencies for FDI prioritisation in ASEAN and OECD countries. Indicators to prioritise low-carbon FDI can be very diverse from one agency to the other – depending on the priorities but also the resources and capacities of these agencies – and are often still in development. Several more sophisticated mechanisms are emerging and increasingly used, however (Box 3.1).

Box 3.1. Environmental sustainability KPIs for prioritisation in selected ASEAN and OECD IPAs

Different indicators have been developed and are used differently by IPAs. Many of them set a target and track the number of attracted and realised projects according to their target sectors and countries.

IDA Ireland has set a target to win 60 environmental sustainability investments in 2021-24. In identifying priority investments, IDA has developed an approach guided by the six sustainable activities set out in the European Union taxonomy on sustainable investment and by an analysis of the sustainability opportunities which align with Ireland's core strengths, and which are deemed to present the greatest opportunity to win FDI.

Business Sweden has embraced the long-term national 'Pioneer the Fossil Free' initiative, by setting clear objectives to accelerate green investments to Sweden to become fossil free by 2045. The agency identifies companies, solutions and expertise that can support reducing CO2 emissions in Sweden and monitors and adapts its investment promotion priorities and activities accordingly.

The *Malaysian Investment Development Authority* targets companies that adopt green technologies and the reuse and recycling of activities, as well as projects applying the circular economy model (e.g. pollution and waste management) to prioritise investment. The *Philippine Board of Investments* uses indicators to prioritise investors with green processes and the use of modern and clean technology.

Some agencies are also developing sustainability scoring mechanisms. For example, *Germany Trade & Invest* developed an integrated scoring model, where FDI projects are assessed and scored against a set of qualitative and quantitative indicators for sustainability. The agency then adjusts its promotion and advisory services to investors accordingly. Similarly, *Invest in Canada* has recently introduced a scoring mechanism to prioritise investment opportunities based on two dimensions: FDI impact and investment potential. The former evaluates the likelihood that the investment will benefit Canada and one variable focuses on social and sustainable development. The agency uses Bloomberg terminal and its scoring system to measure Environmental, Social and Governance (ESG) related impact.

Source: OECD survey on IPA monitoring & evaluation and prioritisation (OECD countries, 2021); direct interactions with IPAs.

To ensure that prioritisation is effective, it is important to have a strong M&E system with relevant indicators. While it is key to prioritise certain investments over others to respond to sustainability objectives, it is equally important to understand and track their contribution to the desired outcomes. Integrating sustainability indicators in IPA M&E systems – going beyond metrics relating to the number and value of investment projects or on the number of jobs created (which is still predominantly the case in IPAs) – is necessary to measure the results of the agency and the effective contribution of assisted companies to sustainable development (Sztajerowska and Volpe Martincus, 2021[10]).

In their efforts to achieve the SDGs through FDI, SADC Member States need to ensure that the actual indicators used by their IPAs to prioritise investments and to measure their outcomes are aligned with the overarching investment promotion priorities. Effective sustainable investment promotion strategies require granular indicators and measurements. Additionally, KPIs used for M&E should ideally be aligned with those used for prioritisation to ensure consistency between the set targets and the desired outcomes.

References

Knoerich, J. and S. Vitting (2021), *The distinct contribution of investment promotion agencies' branch offices in bringing Chinese multinationals to Europe*, Journal of World Business, https://doi.org/10.1016/j.jwb.2020.101187. [4]

OECD (2023), "Enabling sustainable investment in ASEAN", *OECD Business and Finance Policy Papers*, No. 23, OECD Publishing, Paris, https://doi.org/10.1787/eb34f287-en. [8]

OECD (2022), "The geography of foreign investment in OECD member countries: How investment promotion agencies support regional development", *OECD Business and Finance Policy Papers*, No. 20, OECD Publishing, Paris, https://doi.org/10.1787/1f293a25-en. [9]

OECD (2021), *Middle East and North Africa Investment Policy Perspectives*, OECD Publishing, Paris, https://doi.org/10.1787/6d84ee94-en. [3]

OECD (2020), *Investment promotion agencies in the time of COVID-19*, OECD Publishing, https://read.oecd-ilibrary.org/view/?ref=132_132715-6ewiabvnx7&title=Investment-promotion-agencies-in-the-time-of-COVID-19. [5]

OECD (2018), *Mapping of Investment Promotion Agencies*, OECD Publishing, https://www.oecd.org/investment/investment-policy/mapping-of-investment-promotion-agencies-in-OECD-countries.pdf. [1]

OECD (2015), *Policy Framework for Investment, 2015 Edition*, OECD Publishing, Paris, https://doi.org/10.1787/9789264208667-en. [11]

SADC (2006), *Protocol on Finance and Investment*, https://www.sadc.int/sites/default/files/2021-08/Protocol_on_Finance__Investment2006.pdf. [6]

Sauvant, K. and H. Mann (2017), *Towards an Indicative List of FDI Sustainability Characteristics*, https://ssrn.com/abstract=3055961. [2]

Sztajerowska, M. and C. Volpe Martincus (2021), *Together or Apart: Investment Promotion Agencies' Prioritisation and Monitoring and Evaluation for Sustainable Investment Promotion*, OECD Investment Insights, Paris, https://www.oecd.org/daf/inv/investment-policy/Investment-Insights-Investment-Promotion-Prioritisation-OECD.pdf. [10]

UNCTAD (2022), *Commodities at a glance: Special issue on industrial hemp*, UNCTAD, https://unctad.org/system/files/official-document/ditccom2022d1_en.pdf. [7]

Notes

[1] In collaboration with the OECD, a SADC Investment Policy Framework was developed in 2012 to answer the call for specific regional guidance to facilitate co-ordinated approaches on investment frameworks in support of regional development integration. The Framework, inspired by the internationally recognised principles of the OECD Policy Framework for Investment (OECD, 2015[11]), provides country experiences and international good practices to encourage regionally co-ordinated strategies on investment legislative frameworks, promotion and facilitation.

4 Assessing use and design of investment incentives

This chapter looks at tax incentive design and policy goals within SADC and compared to peer regions, based on an analysis of CIT incentives in the 16 SADC Member States. The analysis is based on comparable data from the OECD Investment Tax Incentive Database, covering CIT incentives across 53 developing and emerging countries.

Introduction

SADC governments offer a range of tax incentives in an effort to attract private investment and direct it toward certain sectors, locations, and activities. While tax incentives may promote investments that contribute to advancing the Sustainable Development Goals (SDGs), their benefits and costs are often not well understood. Tax incentives reduce revenue-raising capacity, and can create economic distortions, increase administrative and compliance costs, and increase tax competition. Striking the right balance between a tax regime that supports domestic and foreign investment and securing the necessary revenues for public spending is a challenge for policy makers, particularly in developing countries, where corporate income tax (CIT) revenues are often an important source of public finances.

This chapter looks at tax incentive design and policy goals within SADC and compared to peer regions, based on an analysis of CIT incentives in the 16 SADC Member States. The analysis is based on comparable data from the OECD Investment Tax Incentive Database, covering CIT incentives across 53 developing and emerging economies (Box 4.1). Granular and comprehensive data are indispensable to improve our understanding of existing tax incentive policies and to enhance the analysis of their impacts, given that their effectiveness and costs are strongly design- and context-specific. Analysis of incentive design can inform assessments of whether incentives support positive economic, social and environmental spillovers, and at what costs.

Box 4.1. OECD Investment Tax Incentives Database

To better understand how tax incentives are used across countries, the OECD Investment Tax Incentives Database (ITID) systematically compiles quantitative and qualitative information on the design of CIT incentives, using a consistent data collection methodology. For each tax incentive, it includes information along three dimensions: instrument-specific design features, eligibility conditions and legal basis. This allows for cross-country comparisons on how countries design their tax incentives and what types of business and project characteristics they target. Celani, Dressler and Wermelinger (2022[1]) present the methodology, scope and key classifications underlying the OECD ITID.

As of October 2022, the database covered 53 developing economies in Eurasia, the Middle East and North Africa, Southeast Asia, Sub-Saharan African and includes five LAC economies. The regional groups and corresponding countries included in this report the following:

- *Association of Southeast Asian Nations (ASEAN)*: Cambodia, Indonesia, Lao PDR, Malaysia, Myanmar, Philippines, Thailand, Viet Nam.
- *Eastern Partnership (EaP)*: Armenia, Azerbaijan, Georgia, Moldova, Ukraine.
- *Economic Community of West African States (ECOWAS)*: Cote d'Ivoire, Gambia, Ghana, Liberia, Nigeria, Senegal, Sierra Leone.
- *Latin America and the Caribbean (LAC)*: Argentina, Brazil, Dominican Republic, Jamaica, and Paraguay.
- *Southern African Development Community (SADC)*: All 16 SADC Member States.

Source: Celani, Dressler and Wermelinger (2022[1]), https://doi.org/10.1787/62e075a9-en; OECD (2022[2]), www.oecd.org/investment/investment-policy/oecd-investment-tax-incentives-database-2022-update-brochure.pdf.

Investment tax incentives: opportunities and challenges

In a context of volatile foreign direct investment (FDI) to SADC Member States, most governments consider investment incentives (primarily fiscal but also financial, in-kind and regulatory) as a key tool to promote FDI. The benefits and costs of tax incentives are not always clear. In the best case, tax incentives help attract investors that would not otherwise enter the market, help correct market failures, and encourage positive spillovers of investment on the economy, society or the environment. In the worst cases, incentives result in windfall gains to projects that would have materialised without the incentive, encourage rent-seeking behaviour and distort markets, while costing the state significant resources in foregone revenues, which could be used to advance development aims. Assessing the benefits of incentives and whether they outweigh their direct and indirect costs is not always straightforward.

Whether tax incentives are effective at attracting investors or encouraging positive investor behaviour depends on the country context including the wider investment climate, the investor and project sensitivity to incentives over other location determinants, and the design of the incentive regime (Box 4.2). Investment tax incentives are one, and often not the determining, factor for firms' investment decisions, and cannot compensate for a weak investment climate (Van Parys and James, 2010[3]; Klemm and Van Parys, 2012[4]). Yet, governments often use incentives in place of more difficult reforms, for example, as a way around inefficient tax administration burdens faced by businesses. In some SADC countries, estimates suggest that firms spend on average more than 280 hours to comply with taxes (double the time spent in OECD countries) (PwC, 2020[5]). This can incentivise firms to seek, and governments to grant, tax exemptions to avoid such long procedures, which in turn perpetuates parallel tax treatment that is neither effective nor efficient.

Box 4.2. Context matters for tax incentive effectiveness

In addition to incentive design (covered through this chapter), the effect of tax incentives on investment depends on the characteristics of the investor and country-specific context. Some investors appear to be more sensitive to incentives than others. Projects that privilege low-cost production sites, including some export-oriented manufacturing, and investors that are highly mobile can rank incentives high on factors for location decisions. Other investors, such as those interested in the domestic market or natural resources, appear less swayed by incentives (James, 2014[6]; Andersen, Kett and von Uexkull, 2018[7]).

But investor responsiveness varies by country. Several empirical studies found no effect of tax incentives on FDI attraction in many countries in sub-Saharan Africa (Klemm and Van Parys, 2012[4]; Van Parys and James, 2010[3]; Ghrara and El Morchid, 2022[8]; USAID, 2004[9]). In many developing countries, the quality of infrastructure and the regulatory framework are cited by investors as more important factors in determining their investment location decision than tax benefits (UNIDO, 2013[10]; IMF-OECD, 2017[11]). While lower effective tax rates are associated with higher FDI flows, this effect is significantly stronger in countries with good investment climates, and can have almost no effect in economies with weak investment climates, underlining the importance of wider reforms for FDI attraction (James, 2014[6]).

In general, evidence suggests that while tax benefits can play a role in some investment decisions, they are not necessarily the most effective or efficient policy instrument to stimulate investment (IMF-OECD-UN-World Bank, 2015[12]). Tax competition across countries means that many incentives are overly generous, with costs outweighing the marginal impact on investment (Chai and Goyal, 2008[13]). This underscores the importance of monitoring and evaluating incentive policies.

Across sub-Saharan Africa, the scope of CIT incentives has contributed to an overall narrowing of the corporate income tax base (Keen and Mansour, 2009[14]; Abbas and Klemm, 2013[15]). Statutory CIT rates in most SADC Member States are between 25% and 30%, with a few countries offering lower rates (Mauritius sets the lowest rate at 15%), and three countries (Comoros, DRC, Zambia) setting higher rates (35%). The average rate in the region is similar to that in other developing and emerging regions covered by the database. Yet, incentives can reduce these rates substantially, and many companies may be eligible for them. Analysis of effective average tax rates (EATRs) in five SADC Member States found that CIT incentives on average lowered EATRs by 30-55% compared to the statutory CIT rate in the food and automotive industry, and by as much as 99% in SEZs in Eswatini (Box 4.5).[1]

Meanwhile, tax revenues are a key source of public finances, and are critical for delivering public goods and services (like infrastructure, education and health care), which also affect a country's investment climate. Excessive tax relief for investment projects might limit revenue-mobilising capacity and reduce public resources necessary for progressing towards the SDGs. Public resource mobilisation from taxation is a particular challenge in some SADC Member States; for example, Botswana, the Democratic Republic of Congo (DRC), Madagascar and Malawi all have tax-to-GDP ratios below 15%, which is considered a minimum target rate for growth and development (OECD/ATAF/AUC, 2022[16]; Gaspar, Jaramillo and Wingender, 2016[17]).

The estimated costs of tax incentives are often not transparent, due in part to limited reporting. Evidence from five SADC Member States suggests that estimated foregone CIT revenues (i.e. tax expenditure from CIT incentives) as a share of GDP are low (<0.5%) compared to the OECD average (0.7%). Nevertheless, the impact on overall tax revenues may be higher since CIT revenues account for a larger share of total tax revenues in SADC compared to the OECD (Figure 4.1) (OECD, 2023[18]). For example, in the Seychelles CIT revenue makes up 18% of total tax revenues, more than double the OECD average, while CIT revenue forgone relative to GDP is similar to many OECD countries, and above that of peers. In Eswatini, Madagascar, Seychelles and DRC tax incentives on goods and services (including VAT, customs duties and excise tax) cost up to double in terms of revenue forgone than CIT incentives, showing the importance of looking at the full scope of tax benefits available to investors in considering their costs and their contribution to achieving policy goals (Redonda, von Haldenwang and Aliu, 2022[19]).[2]

Figure 4.1. Tax expenditure can be costly even when dependency on CIT revenues high

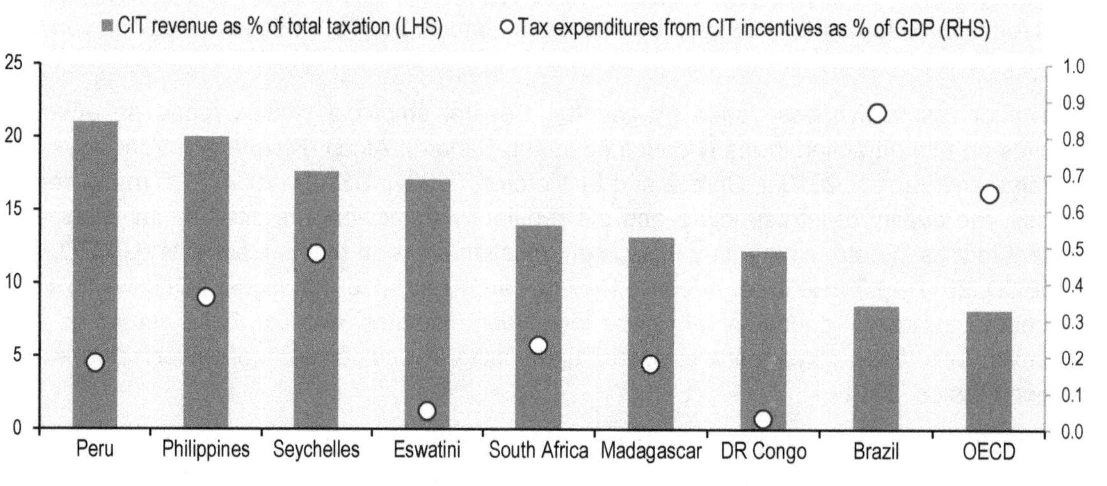

Note: CIT revenue as share of total tax revenue for year 2020; estimated tax expenditures from CIT incentives as a percentage of GDP for year 2020 except Madagascar (2021), Eswatini (2017), and DRC (2018).
Source: OECD Global Revenue Statistics and Global Tax Expenditures Database (2023[18]) (Redonda, von Haldenwang and Aliu, 2022[19]).

Many governments are aware of the costs and unclear benefits of incentives, but face high pressure to offer generous incentive packages, internally from firms lobbying for advantages, and externally from competition with other countries with generous regimes. Analysis of the scope, goals and design of incentives is key, as improving design can help limit redundancies and encourage positive spillovers. Conditioning incentives on specific outcomes or promoting these outcomes through other eligibility criteria, while limiting the generosity of some incentives can be an important step in this regard. It is expected that the global minimum tax, agreed by 138 jurisdictions, will also help curb harmful tax competition, and encourage better incentive design (Box 4.4).

Tax incentive design in SADC: insights from the OECD ITID

Tax incentive design is a key determinant of the effectiveness and costs of incentives. It relates to how the incentive reduces taxation (the instrument and the qualifying income or expenditures it applies to, and other features (Box 4.3)), eligibility conditions (which investors and projects qualify to receive the incentive), and governance (how the incentive is awarded to investors) (Celani, Dressler and Wermelinger, 2022[1]). These policy design choices determine incentive targeting and affect incentive uptake, the extent to which incentives contribute to stated policy goals, and at what cost. The OECD ITID provides insights into how SADC Member States use and grant incentives, which policy goals they seek to achieve, and how these practices compare with other regional groups. This analysis should be considered in conjunction with other chapters of this review, including how incentives factor into investment promotion strategies and whether incentives are prevalent in sectors already receiving FDI.

Box 4.3. Common tax incentive instruments

Investment tax incentives provide favourable deviations from the standard tax treatment for a specific group of corporate taxpayers, based on sector, activity, location or other investor- or project-related characteristics. Most countries provide preferential CIT treatment through four main instruments:

Tax exemptions provide a full or partial exemption of qualifying taxable income, which may refer to all of a business' income or income from specific sources (e.g. export income).

Reduced rates provide CIT rates below the standard (statutory) rate for qualifying taxable income.

Tax allowances and **tax credits** allow firms to deduct a certain share of qualifying capital or current expenditure from taxable income (tax allowances) or directly from taxes due (tax credits). Qualifying capital expenditures are generally asset specific (e.g. machinery, buildings, equipment). Qualifying current expenditure tends to be activity specific (e.g. spending on training, R&D, exporting). Tax allowances on capital expenditure can accelerate or enhance the deduction of capital costs. Tax allowances that accelerate the deduction of capital costs allow for the faster recovery of the cost of an asset, while tax allowances that enhance deductions apply in addition to standard capital deductions (available to all taxpayers) and result in deductions that effectively exceed the initial capital cost. Tax allowances on current expenditures and tax credits can result in deductions that effectively exceed original expenses (for example, a 200% tax allowance on employee training).

The first two instruments (tax exemptions and reduced rates) are **income-based incentives**; they provide tax relief based on earnings. Tax allowances and credits are **expenditure-based incentives** because they lower the cost of capital or certain spending.

Source: Celani, Dressler and Wermelinger (2022[1]), https://doi.org/10.1787/62e075a9-en.

Use of expenditure-based incentives growing among SADC Member States

While income-based incentives (i.e. CIT exemptions and reduced CIT rates) are widely used across developing economies, these incentives are not always effective in attracting new investment, and have substantial costs – including forgone tax revenue, economic distortions and increased tax competition – which could outweigh their benefits (IMF-OECD-UN-World Bank, 2015[12]; James, 2014[6]; Zee, Stotsky and Ley, 2002[20]). Income-based incentives disproportionately benefit projects that are already profitable early in the tax relief period, making projects that could materialise without the incentive even more profitable. CIT exemptions are particularly costly, and can result in race-to-the-bottom tax competition with other economies over mobile foreign investment, while potentially generating windfall gains for projects that would have taken place in absence of the incentives (Klemm and Van Parys, 2012[4]; James, 2014[6]). CIT exemptions and reduced CIT rates are likely to be particularly affected by the global minimum tax (Box 4.4).

Box 4.4. Tax incentives and the global minimum tax for MNEs

The recently agreed Global Minimum Tax for large MNEs places multilaterally limits to tax competition that contribute to the erosion of domestic tax bases. Pillar Two of the two-pillar solution agreed by 138 members of the Inclusive Framework on Base Erosion and Profit Shifting requires large MNEs (with revenues above USD 750 million) to pay a 15% minimum effective tax rate in all jurisdictions in which they operate. This means that if there are affiliates of an in scope MNEs with an effective tax rates (ETR) below 15%, top-up taxes may be due. In the absence of tax reform or other policy actions, governments could potentially forgo such revenues arising from low-taxed profit in their jurisdiction that would be collected by other jurisdictions.

As more countries are moving to implement the global minimum tax, it is important for ECOWAS Member States to analyse the implications of the global minimum tax on domestic tax systems. The GloBE Rules will not affect all jurisdictions, MNEs and tax incentives in the same manner. The impact of the GloBE Rules on tax incentives will depend on their design, on the jurisdiction's tax system (its baseline tax system and its use of base narrowing provisions), and on the characteristics of MNEs and the activities they perform in the jurisdiction.

The impact of the GloBE Rules will strongly depend on the design of tax incentives. OECD analysis shows that income-based incentives for in-scope MNEs will be strongly affected, whereas expenditure-based incentives are less likely to be affected, with some incentives such as accelerated depreciation for tangible assets affected only to a limited extent. The new rules allow a carve-out for profits associated with economic substance (the substance-based income exclusion, SBIE), which allows 5% of the value of tangible assets and payroll to be subtracted from the profits to which the top-up tax applies. This means that tax incentives that are successful in attracting tangible assets and generating employment will be less affected from the minimum tax.

Governments are strongly advised to consider the implications of the minimum tax on their tax incentives. It will be important to ensure coordination across ministries on this issue given the fast pace of action of reform in this area.

Source: OECD (2022[21]), https://doi.org/10.1787/25d30b96-en.

There is evidence suggesting potential positive effects of expenditure-based incentives on investment under certain conditions (House and Shapiro, 2008[22]; Appelt, González Cabral and Hanappi, 2022[23]). Because expenditure-based incentives directly target investment expenses, they reduce the cost of capital, making investments more profitable at the margin (IMF, OECD, UN, World Bank, 2015[24]). The benefit for the company depends on the size of the investment it undertakes and can also be linked to spending on specific activities and policy objectives (e.g. R&D, skills development). These incentives therefore lend themselves to improving the positive impact of investment on sustainable development (OECD, 2022[25]). Additional research is required to assess impacts in different contexts. Expenditure-based incentives typically have higher administrative costs, and if not well designed can favour existing companies over new ventures with low profits (UN-CIAT, 2018[26]; Morisset and Pirnia, 1999[27]). All incentives require comprehensive monitoring and evaluation to assess their costs and benefits.

Income-based instruments (CIT exemptions and reduced rates) are most commonly used across the region. Each SADC Member State offers at least one type of income-based CIT incentive: 15 countries offer at least one reduced CIT rate, and six countries provide at least one tax reduction to 0% rate; Out of ten countries that offer CIT exemptions to investors, eight provide at least one full CIT exemption. Most tax exemptions and reduced rates target specific sectors, primarily manufacturing, agriculture and services. Around one-third of income-based benefits are for firms in special economic zones (SEZs). Nevertheless, the use of these income-based instruments is less ubiquitous than in most other regions covered by the dataset (Figure 4.2). Many countries have undertaken reforms to limit full tax exemptions and reductions. The DRC is the only SADC country that uses only income-based incentives. All other fifteen SADC Member States use at least one tax allowances in their incentive mix to attract investors (Figure 4.2). Seven of the 16 countries offer mostly expenditure-based incentives (tax allowances and credits), primarily targeted to initial capital expenditure. Eleven countries offer tax allowances for current expenditure, including costs related to training, R&D, and job creation. South Africa and the Seychelles use almost only expenditure-based tax incentives. In general, expenditure-based incentives are more commonly used by countries with higher income levels given their greater capacity requirements in terms of administration and compliance monitoring.

Figure 4.2. SADC countries offer a mix of income- and expenditure-based incentives

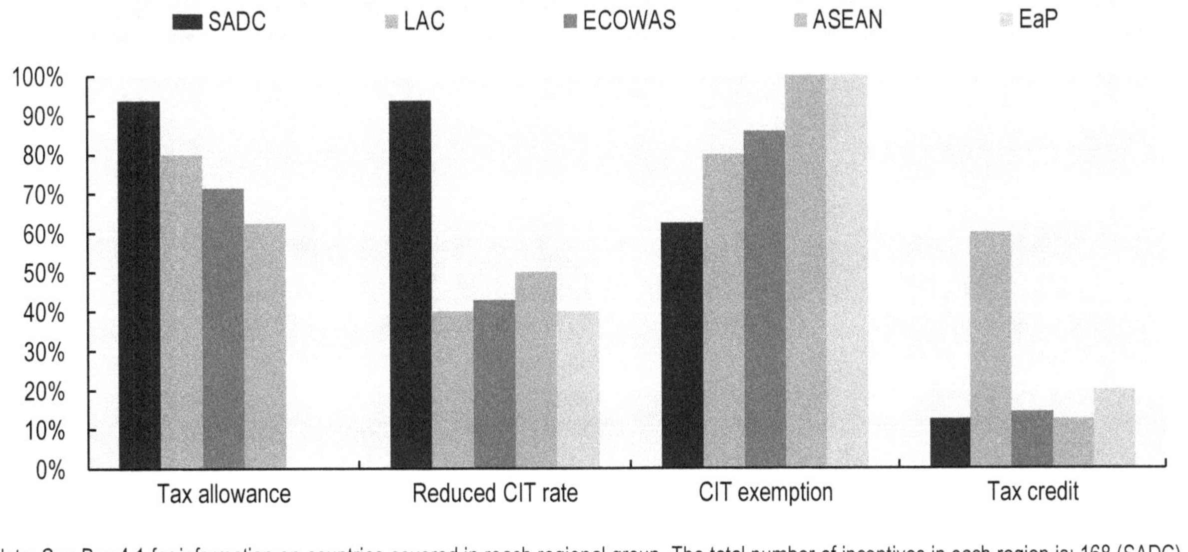

Note: See Box 4.1 for information on countries covered in reach regional group. The total number of incentives in each region is: 168 (SADC), 69 (ECOWAS), 78 (ASEAN), 19 (EaP), 38 (LAC).
Source: OECD ITID, April 2023, based on 53 economies and 482 CIT incentive entries.

While many countries (across regions) offer permanent low CIT rates for certain sectors, these benefits are costly in terms of revenue forgone as well as potential long-term economic distortions. Stability is important to investors, but when incentive recipients gain permanent preferential treatment vis-à-vis competitors, incentives can become a tool for rent-seeking (Abramovsky et al., 2018[28]) (Lent, 1967[29]). Permanently reduced rates should be assessed for generosity compared to the statutory rate (see Box 4.5 on ETRs). Temporary incentives, and especially full CIT exemptions, also have costs and risks, including that firms will leave the jurisdiction when the incentive expires. Some firms may also use tactics to continue receiving the incentive after their benefit has lapsed, such as by incorporating a new firm that qualifies for the CIT exemption, creating de-facto permanent incentives (IMF-OECD-UN-World Bank, 2015[12]).

The majority of income-based incentives granted in SADC are temporary, in line with good practice. For example, Mauritius offers an eight-year CIT exemption for manufacturers of pharmaceuticals, medical devices and high-tech products. Half of the income-based incentives in SADC are granted for periods of five to ten years, and around a quarter are granted permanently (Figure 4.3). Duration of these incentives is similar to ECOWAS and ASEAN, though ASEAN offers relatively more short-term incentives (under five years) and very few permanent benefits, while ECOWAS offers relatively few incentives for periods over ten years. The trend at the SADC Member State level is similar: most offer predominantly income-based incentives for ten years or less; two-thirds of countries also offer some permanent benefits, which are primarily reduced CIT rates for certain industries, such as manufacturers with majority of turnover from exports (Zimbabwe) or farming and food processing (Zambia); there are very few examples of permanent CIT exemptions. It is noteworthy that Namibia has been phasing out all CIT exemptions (including permanent ones) available to firms in Export Processing Zones since 2020.

Figure 4.3. Most income-based incentives are granted for 5-10 years

Duration of income-based incentives, as a share of total number of income-based incentives in each region (as covered by the database)

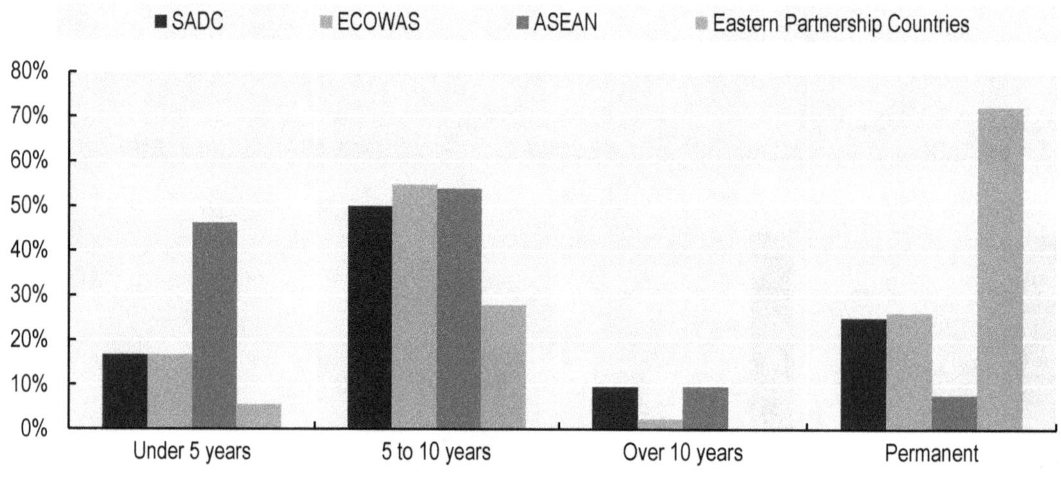

Note: See Box 4.1 for information on countries covered in reach regional group. The graph reflects durations of CIT exemptions and reduced CIT rates. The number of income-based incentives reflected in each region is: 84 (SADC), 42 (ECOWAS), 52 (ASEAN), 18 (EaP).
Source: OECD ITID, April 2023, based on 53 economies and 482 CIT incentive entries.

Six SADC Member States have at least one incentive with a sunset clause. Sunset clauses stipulate an end date to an incentive policy unless legislative action is taken to extend the benefit. Most CIT incentives in South Africa have sunset clauses, including a phase out of reduced CIT rates in SEZs, and a tax allowance for industrial projects Temporary benefits could encourage monitoring and evaluation, as the merits of an incentive can be assessed after a fixed period to determine whether the incentive should be continued, reformed or left to expire, particularly if evaluation requirements are in the law. Moreover, they can also be easier to remove, as politically it is often more difficult for governments to end incentives than to introduce new ones. Lastly, there is some evidence that expenditure-based tax incentives with a sunset clause may have a greater effect on investment attraction than permanent benefits, since investors are encouraged to act quickly to enjoy the benefit (Wen, 2020[30]; US Department of the Treasury, 2010[31]). However, governments must clearly communicate if incentives are time-bound, as sunset clauses can introduce an element of uncertainty for investors.

Eligibility conditions suggest focus on manufacturing and other key sectors

Incentive eligibility conditions are criteria that businesses or investment projects must meet to receive a tax benefit. Incentive policies often tie tax support to investment in specific sectors or locations, or certain investor or project characteristics (e.g. majority foreign-owned, minimum investment value, new entrant). Incentives are also often conditional on certain investor activities (e.g. training, R&D) or outcomes (e.g. job creation, energy efficiency) (Celani, Dressler and Wermelinger, 2022[1]). In SADC, sector-related criteria are by far the most commonly used (in all 16 countries), followed be SEZ criteria (used by 12 countries) which is similar to practices observed in other economies (Figure 4.4, Panel A.). Over half of the incentives granted by SADC Member States require investors to meet only one eligibility condition to benefit (Figure 4.4). When multiple eligibility conditions are used, sector conditions are often combined with requirements to invest in a certain region or SEZ, or meet a certain outcome.

Figure 4.4. Most incentives target certain sectors, often as the only eligibility condition

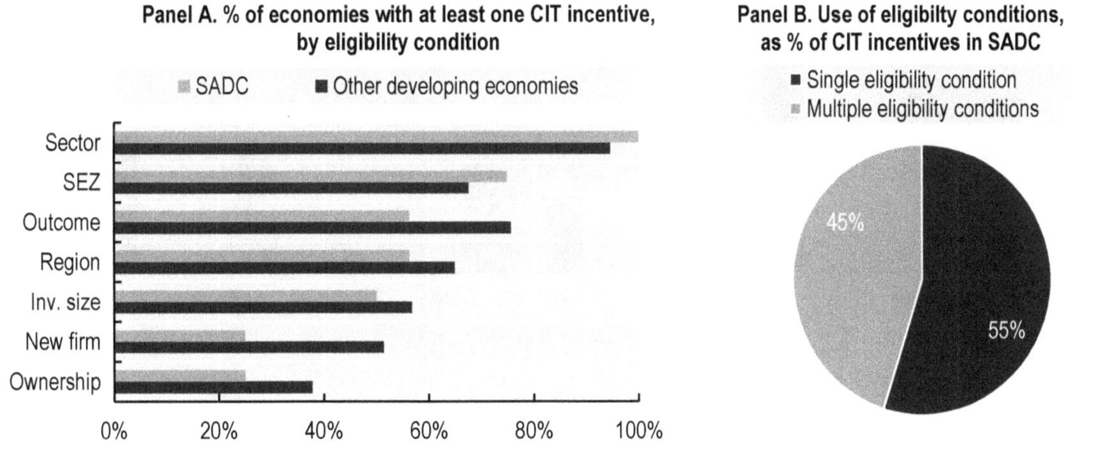

Note: Panel B reflects 144 CIT incentives registered in the OECD ITID with at least one eligibility condition. The number of incentives that have specific eligibility criteria is 144 (SADC) and 302 (Other developing economies). Shares do not add up to 100% because incentives can have multiple eligibility criteria.
Source: OECD ITID, April 2023, based on 53 economies and 482 CIT incentive entries.

All 16 SADC Member States offer incentives conditional on sector of activity. Most of these define eligible sectors in a positive list (the focus of this section). Sector targeting can be broad (e.g. if the incentive is available to investors active in the entire manufacturing or agricultural sector) or narrow (only available to projects in a set of sub-sectors, e.g. temporary reduced CIT rate for production of pharmaceuticals and leather industry in Tanzania). Broad sector categories are agriculture, mining and quarrying, manufacturing, electricity/water/waste, and services.

More than one third of incentives in SADC support investors in manufacturing (36%), followed by agriculture (29%) and services (23%) (Figure 4.5). This means that incentives are available to investors operating in these broad sector categories or in a subset of industries. For manufacturing, two-thirds of SADC Member States have incentives that support the entire manufacturing sector; ten countries target food and beverage manufacturing; a third of SADC countries targets a range of other industries, and including textiles, chemicals and plastics, and electrical equipment. While only 23% of all incentives target services, which is a much lower share than in ASEAN but in line with ECOWAS, these incentives are offered by over two-thirds of SADC countries. Angola, Mozambique and Madagascar target the most diverse set of services. The service sub-sector most frequently targeted (by 9 countries) is tourism, followed by infrastructure (5 countries). Just 9% of incentives in SADC target mining and quarrying industries (including coal, oil and gas, metal ore and other mining), less than other comparator regions. In line with best practice, most of these incentives are accelerated allowances to support high initial capital costs, while there are few examples of CIT exemptions for extractive industries, which can be both ineffective at attracting additional investment and inefficient (i.e. costs are greater than benefits) (IGF-OECD, 2018[32]; James, 2014[6]). Four SADC Member States offer incentives for investments in renewable energy.

Figure 4.5. Sector-based incentives primarily support manufacturing

% of incentives registered in the OECD ITID

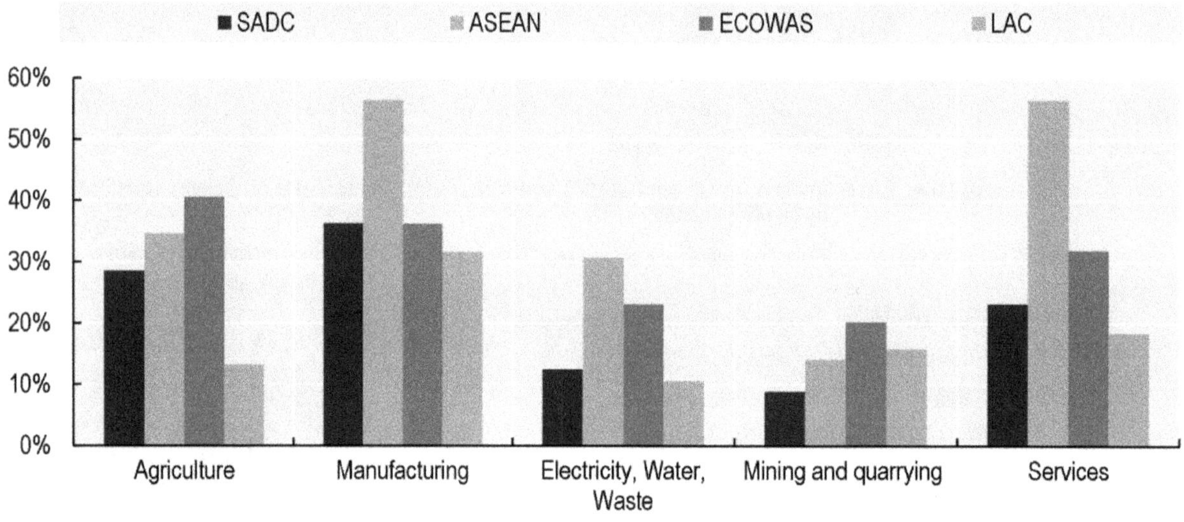

Note: See Box 4.1 for information on countries covered in reach regional group. The number of registered incentives in each region is: 168 (SADC), 69 (ECOWAS), 78 (ASEAN), 38 (LAC). Incentives can be specific to one or more sub-sectors within these five sector categories, or are available to any investor that falls under the broad category. Shares do not add up to 100% as incentives can target multiple sectors.
Source: OECD ITID, April 2023, based on 53 economies and 482 CIT incentive entries.

Overall, sector-based incentives in SADC are more targeted than in other regions like ECOWAS and ASEAN. Just over a third of sector-based incentives target multiple broad sector categories (e.g. agriculture and manufacturing) at once; these incentives are usually for investors in SEZs that seek to support, for example, manufacturing and some services industries. By comparison, countries in ASEAN and ECOWAS offer a greater share of incentives to investors across multiple broad sectors. This reflects a difference in the mode and extent of targeting. Other regions tend to target beneficiaries by location or minimum investment value, whereas SADC appears to have a stronger focus on supporting specific industries. Industry targeting can be a means of containing costs of incentives by focusing only on priority activities, which are expected to create the greatest economic, social and environmental benefits (Celani,

Dressler and Wermelinger, 2022[1]). However, the benefits and costs of narrow versus broad sector targeting are not thoroughly assessed in the literature.

Investment location is a common condition

Investment location is the second most frequently used eligibility criterion for incentives offered in SADC, as is the case in other developing regions (Figure 4.4, Panel A). At the Member State level, all but two SADC countries (Lesotho and Seychelles, both geographically smaller countries) offer at least one incentive for investors that locate in a specific region or economic zone. Investing in an economic zone is required for at least one CIT incentive in 12 out of 16 countries, while investing in a specific (non-zone) subnational location is required in 9 SADC Member States. Location-based incentives generally give greater benefits to investments outside of capital cities, and often in less developed areas. For example, Mozambique provides an enhanced allowance for costs related to infrastructure, utilities, or other investments considered public goods outside Maputo. Angola and DRC divide their countries into different zones, with preferential benefits in more remote areas. Three-quarters of SADC Member States use SEZs, including industrial zones, free ports, and export processing zones. According to an assessment of EATRs in a sample of SADC Member States, incentives in SEZs typically offer the most generous tax treatment (Box 4.5).

Box 4.5. Estimated EATRs in Sub-Saharan Africa suggest generous benefits in SEZs

Forward-looking corporate effective average tax rates (EATRs) are a way of measuring the extent to which tax incentives affect tax costs and influence business investment and location decisions. Using the OECD's forward-looking corporate EATR framework, a comparison was made on how CIT incentives affect EATRs in seven Sub-Saharan African countries (Angola, Botswana, Eswatini, Kenya, Mauritius, Senegal and South Africa) in two sectors – food and automotive industries – and in Special Economic Zones (SEZs).

Across the seven Sub-Saharan African countries, tax incentives reduce EATRs by 30% on average in the sectors considered. The most generous tax treatment is typically offered within SEZs, where ETRs are reduced on average by 65% compared to the standard tax treatment. In some specific cases, including in Eswatini and Mauritius, tax incentives can reduce EATRs to nearly zero.

A range of different EATRs is applicable within each country, depending on the sectors, locations and projects targeted by the incentives. Even within sectors, different EATRs often apply due to varying investor or project characteristics (e.g. project size, profitability, the taxable income position over the lifetime of the project), specific incentive design provisions (e.g. benefit ceilings, treatment of carry-forwards, etc.) and interactions of incentives with standard capital allowances. These features can substantially affect the size of the tax benefit from incentives. Depending on their design and context, expenditure-based incentives can deliver tax benefits that are as generous as income-based ones.

The findings reveal several – potentially unintended – effects of tax incentive policies on the tax costs of investment and on revenue forgone across the different periods of an investment's lifecycle. This highlights the importance of careful design, including of interactions between incentives.

Source: Celani, Dressler and Hanappi (2022[33])

Outcome conditions focus on domestic value added and export promotion

Outcome conditions require companies to achieve certain performance results to be eligible for a tax incentive. They are linked to the outcome of the investment, rather than the characteristics of the qualifying investor (Celani, Dressler and Wermelinger, 2022[1]). Nine out of 16 SADC countries offer at least one incentive with a specific outcome or performance requirement. The most common performance criteria relate to domestic value added, exports, and jobs created for country nationals. For example, Zimbabwe offers reduced CIT rates for manufacturers that export over 41% of turnover. In Comoros, reduced CIT rates are conditional on number of jobs created per year.

Outcome conditions can be designed to promote positive economic, social and environmental spillovers. For example, in Eswatini, investors in SEZs are required to pay wages that are 90% above the minimum wage to receive a tax exemption. South Africa grants a tax allowance on machinery and training costs if the project meets a combination of (mostly) quantifiable criteria related to energy efficiency, innovation, SME procurement and local linkages. Outcome conditions are, however, often vague or based on non-quantifiable criteria (e.g. contributes to job creation or beneficial to the national economy), leaving ample room for discretionary approval of incentives by awarding authorities. Outcome conditions also require monitoring to ensure that the outcome has been met, which requires public resources, administrative capacity, and often co-ordination with other government agencies (e.g. cross-checking with social security information on number of jobs created or salary).

Some incentives are designed to support economic and other development goals

Many countries use investment incentives in an effort to advance certain economic, social, environmental and other goals. As noted, this can be through incentive eligibility conditions that require investors to meet certain performance criteria (e.g. job creation) or operate in certain sectors (e.g. renewable energy), or by designing the incentive to reduce the costs of certain activities (e.g. R&D, training), and increasing the revenues associated with others (e.g. exports).

The main goals of CIT incentives in SADC are to encourage infrastructure development, exports, and job quality and skills development (by nine out of 16 Member States, respectively) (Figure 4.6, Panel A). Other goals include promoting the green transition (in seven countries, mostly by targeting renewable energy and waste management/recycling), employment and job creation (in six countries) , while few seek to advance social inclusion (in three countries) (Figure 4.6, Panel B). Only South Africa used a tax incentive to promote linkages with the local economy, however, the incentive got recently repealed.[3] Although not illustrated in the figure, some SADC member states also have incentives to support innovation or research and development (e.g. an accelerated depreciation rate of 40% for R&D expenditure in the Seychelles).

Figure 4.6. Most SADC countries target incentives to support sustainable development goals

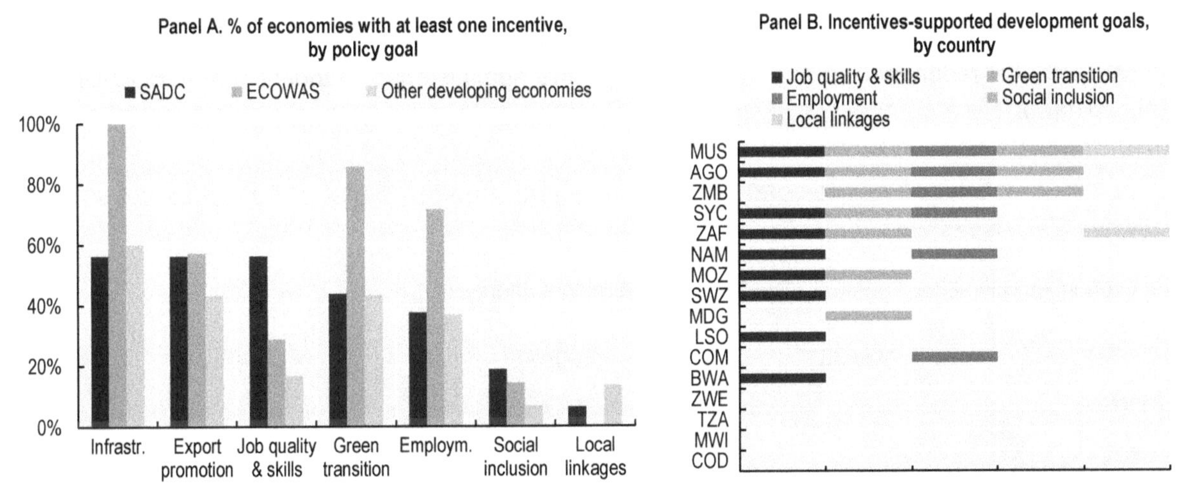

Note: See Box 4.1 for information on countries covered in reach regional group and Annex A for indicator methodology. Panel B indicates that countries support respective SDGs with at least one CIT incentive. The total number of incentives in each region is: 168 (SADC), 69 (ECOWAS), and 245 (other developing regions).
Source: OECD ITID, April 2023, based on 53 economies and 482 CIT incentive entries.

The ITID shows that incentives are used to promote a range of SDGs including quality jobs, skills, green transition and social inclusion. While incentives have the potential to contribute to these goals, the costs of administering and monitoring compliance with stated performance criteria can be high. Furthermore, tax policy or other types of incentives (such as grants or in-kind subsidies) are not the only way to encourage the industrial development or influence investor behaviour, and tax incentives should at most be complementary to other policy tools (OECD, 2022[25]).

Three-quarters of SADC Member States tie at least some of their incentives to SDGs (Figure 4.6, Panel B) Most of these incentives are tax allowances that seek to stimulate a behaviour by lowering its relative costs, for example encouraging job creation. Angola, Mauritius and Zambia offer enhanced tax allowances for costs of salaries or other emoluments (e.g. pensions contributions) for employment of disabled workers. Angola provides deductions for new jobs created for women. The Seychelles offers allowances for hiring national employees from technical and vocational training institutions for technology, farming, maritime and tourism. A number of countries offer incentives that support the green transition:

Mauritius and the Seychelles provide accelerated depreciation for machinery and equipment to generate renewable energy and increase energy efficiency; Madagascar provides a tax allowance of 50% of investment costs for the renewable energy sector; South Africa used to provide a tax deduction of 95 cents per kilowatt hour of verified energy efficiency savings;[4] Angola taxes income from sale of renewable energy at a reduced rate. Monitoring and evaluation are key to assess whether these incentives support stated goals.

Most incentives are granted by the Ministry of Finance

Governance of incentives includes how tax benefits are authorised in laws or regulations and awarded to investors. It also concerns whether incentives are transparent, and whether eligibility conditions to receive incentives are clear and specific, or based on interpretation and approval from administering authorities. Governance also involves how compliance with incentive conditions is monitored and incentive policies evaluated ex-post.

Most SADC Member States introduce tax incentives via the tax law and them through the Ministry of Finance (Figure 4.7). The Ministry of Finance is often best placed to grant incentives and monitor their costs. Other ministries or agencies may be more inclined to offer fiscal benefits as they are not in charge of tax collection or necessarily aware of the state's fiscal needs (James, 2014[6]). There is broad international consensus that consolidating all tax incentives in tax laws enhances transparency and reduces potential redundancies and confusion over the administering authority (IMF-OECD-UN-World Bank, 2015[12]).

Figure 4.7. Most SADC countries grant tax incentives through the Ministry of Finance but some countries also use other authorities/bodies

% of economies with at least one CIT incentive per governing authority

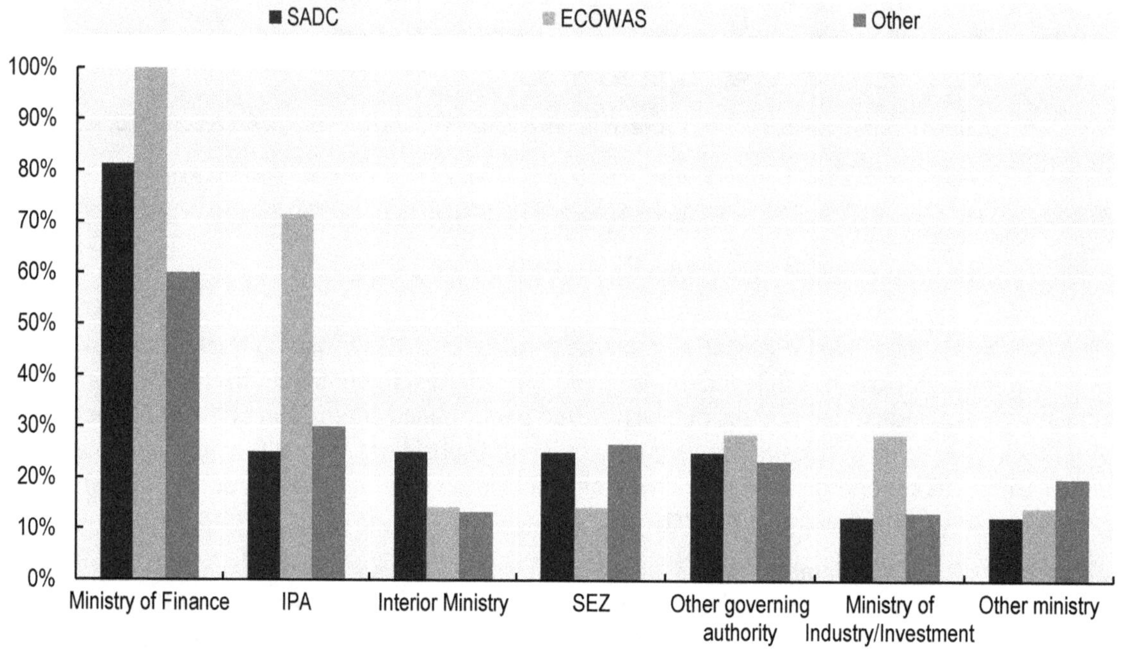

Note: See Box 4.1 for information on countries covered in reach regional group. The number of incentives for which the details of granting authorities are available in each region is 69 (ECOWAS); 168 (SADC); 245 (Other).
Source: OECD ITID, April 2023, based on 53 economies and 482 CIT incentive entries.

Similar to other regions, most SADC Member States also grant some incentives through other government agencies, including investment promotion agencies (IPA), line ministries, and SEZ authorities (Figure 4.7). In half of SADC Member States, different agencies share responsibility for granting at least one incentive. Different agencies can bring valuable insights for incentive design, monitoring and evaluation. But without clear co-ordination incentives may overlap or be inconsistent (IMF-OECD-UN-World Bank, 2015[12]). Administration of incentives by multiple authorities with overlapping responsibilities, can also increase opportunities for aggressive tax planning by investors.

Most CIT incentives in SADC are transparent, in that eligibility criteria to receive the benefit are clearly stated in laws and regulations and tend to be specific (e.g. lists of eligible sectors). However, as in other regions, some incentives offered in SADC are less transparent: either the incentive has broad and less clearly defined eligibility criteria (e.g. contributing to economic development and job creation), or investors may be eligible for additional tax benefits not specified in laws. Some SADC Member States require investors to receive a special certificate, investment licence or industry status, particularly in SEZs, based on an application to relevant authorities. While requirements are usually clear, this is not always the case; applications can also introduce a layer of discretion in awarding incentives.

When granting authorities have wide discretion to determine who can receive incentives and the extent of benefits, it increases the risk of rent-seeking behaviour and corruption, as well as unfair competition between firms (IMF-OECD-UN-World Bank, 2015[12]). The OECD ITID also only covers CIT incentives introduced in legal texts, many countries grant incentives on an ad hoc negotiated basis with investors (e.g. through bilateral contracts); these are by their nature non-transparent. Incentives for specific large oil and gas or mining companies can be granted on a contract basis. Further analysis is required to assess governance across the full life cycle of the incentive, including monitoring and evaluation.

Assessing the impact of incentives: next steps

For governments, better understanding whether incentives contribute to policy goals, and at what costs, requires monitoring and evaluation (M&E), although this requires data and resources that are often not available. Short of more in-depth cost-benefit analysis (including through use of forward-looking ETRs, discussed in Box 4.5), governments can do more to track incentive goals and use. An important first step to create accountability and transparency is identifying and describing all available incentives, their policy goal, and legal reference in publicly available documents. This is particularly important if different agencies are involved in granting incentives. Governments can regularly assess if stated goals of tax incentives (directing investment in particular sectors or activities), align with investment promotion strategies and national development goals.

As a next step, information on incentive uptake and characteristics of beneficiary firms can provide important insights into how incentives are used, and if incentives appear to be supporting projects most in need. Many SADC Member States, as in other regions, require that firms apply to receive benefits. Though this can introduce a risk of discretionary awarding of incentives, if based on clear and specific eligibility criteria, incentive applications could form the basis of initial monitoring. More in-depth monitoring of firm compliance with the terms of the incentive (for example, jobs created, value of exports), can assist in determining if the incentive is contributing to development goals.

To compare how these benefits measure against costs, tax expenditure reports are key to estimate revenue forgone. Based on research by the Global Tax Expenditure Database, seven out of 16 SADC Member States (Madagascar, Mauritius, South Africa, Tanzania, the Democratic Republic of Congo, Lesotho, and the Seychelles) have reported estimates on revenue forgone from tax incentives to the public at least once between 2000 and 2019 (Redonda, von Haldenwang and Aliu, 2022[19]; 2021[34]). Often this information is aggregated as total tax expenditures, without clear descriptions on how estimations are calculated. There are however examples of countries that regularly publish more detailed information, notably Mauritius (which began reporting in 2007) and South Africa (which began in 2011). Tanzania has released a single report covering 12 years of estimates. These are important developments key to both public transparency on costs of incentive programmes and as a first step towards cost-benefit analysis. However, these countries do not publicly report on costs of specific incentives (provision-level data), which is key to assessing performance of different types of incentives (Redonda, Von Haldenwang and Aliu, 2021[34]).

Many governments face challenges to tax expenditure reporting, including resource constraints and lack of co-ordination across agencies involved in granting tax incentives. Some incentives are by their nature more difficult to monitor. Beneficiaries of full CIT exemptions may be exempt from filing tax returns, complicating estimates of costs in revenue forgone (Klemm, 2009[35]). The SADC Tax Subcommittee, in partnership with donors, developed a Tax Expenditure Model in 2015, updated in 2022, to support tax administrations to estimate and analyse tax revenue forgone. It is not clear, however, whether this model is used.

Tax expenditure reporting and monitoring can help identify incentives that are no longer efficient. A few SADC countries provide good examples of such reform. South Africa is phasing out certain tax allowances for industrial projects, including the most generous allowances to projects in SEZs (repealed in March 2020). As of August 2021, Mauritius repealed most of its temporary tax exemptions for new manufacturing businesses (Celani, Dressler and Hanappi, 2022[33]). Namibia repealed full CIT exemptions under its Export Processing Zones at the end of 2020, with transitions for existing companies to a new SEZ regime. Namibia's Finance Minister cited the decision as linked to a review that high costs to the government exceeded sought after benefits in terms of investment and job creation. The reform also complies with EU requirements for removal from the list of non-co-operative jurisdictions for tax purposes (a "blacklist" of tax havens); the EU removed Namibia in February 2021 (Reuters, 2020[36]; Deloitte, 2021[37]).

Deepening co-operation at the regional level on tax incentives use could continue to help reduce tax competition, promote evaluation of policies, and provide guidelines for good governance and transparency. SADC Member States have committed to co-operate on tax incentive policies, including on a common framework to improve the effectiveness of incentives at achieving their policy goals and the impact of tax incentives on revenue costs (as outlined in Annex 3 of the Protocol on Finance and Investment, and in the Memorandum of Understanding on Co-operation in Taxation and Related Matters) (SADC, 2023[38]). There have been notable areas of this co-operation, including, in addition to the Tax Expenditure Model, the creation of an online tax database on all incentives offered – though this has since been removed – and guidelines on co-ordination of VAT and excise regimes. Assessing how Member States are using these tools is an area for further research, as well as how additional frameworks could be developed to guide governments to monitor and evaluate effectiveness of incentive policies. Building on reforms conducted in certain member states could be a starting point for peer-learning.

References

Abbas, S. and A. Klemm (2013), "A partial race to the bottom: Corporate tax developments in emerging and developing economies", *International Tax and Public Finance*, Vol. 20/4, pp. 596-617, https://doi.org/10.1007/S10797-013-9286-8/TABLES/5. [15]

Abramovsky, L. et al. (2018), "Are corporate tax incentives for investment fit for purpose? Revisiting economic principles and evidence from low- and middle-income countries", https://doi.org/10.1920/RE.IFS.2018.0142. [28]

Andersen, M., B. Kett and E. von Uexkull (2018), "Corporate Tax Incentives and FDI in Developing Countries", in *Global Investment Competitiveness Report 2017/2018: Foreign Investor Perspectives and Policy Implications*, World Bank Group, Washington, DC, https://pubdocs.worldbank.org/en/964321508856694021/GICR-03.pdf (accessed on 11 May 2021). [7]

Appelt, S., A. González Cabral and T. Hanappi (2022), "Income-based tax incentives for R&D and innovation: Measures of tax expenditure and uptake", *OECD Science, Technology and Innovation Working Paper series*, OECD, Paris. [23]

ATI-CEP-IDOS (2022), *Workshop Report*, Addis Tax Initiative (ATI), Council on Economic Policies (CEP), German Institute of Development and Sustainability (IDOS), https://www.addistaxinitiative.net/sites/default/files/resources/Report-ATI%20Regional%20Workshop%20%28En%29.pdf (accessed on 5 March 2023). [42]

Celani, A., L. Dressler and T. Hanappi (2022), "Assessing tax relief from targeted investment tax incentives through corporate effective tax rates", *OECD Taxation Working Paper Series*, OECD, Paris, https://doi.org/10.1787/22235558. [33]

Celani, A., L. Dressler and M. Wermelinger (2022), "OECD Investment Tax Incentives Database: Enhancing transparency through comparable data in developing countries", *OECD Working Papers on International Investment*, OECD, Paris, https://doi.org/10.1787/18151957. [1]

Chai, J. and R. Goyal (2008), "Tax Concessions and Foreign Direct Investment in the Eastern Caribbean Currency Union", *IMF Working Papers*, No. 2008/257, International Monetary Fund, https://www.imf.org/en/Publications/WP/Issues/2016/12/31/Tax-Concessions-and-Foreign-Direct-Investment-in-the-Eastern-Caribbean-Currency-Union-22456. [13]

Deloitte (2021), *Deloitte commentary on Namibian Budget 2021/2022*, Deloitte, Windhoek, https://www2.deloitte.com/content/dam/Deloitte/na/Documents/tax/Deloitte_Namibia%20Budget%20Commentary_2021(final)18.03.2021.pdf (accessed on 19 April 2023). [37]

ECOWAS Commission (2018), *ECOWAS Investment Policy*, https://wacomp.projects.ecowas.int/wp-content/uploads/2020/03/ECOWAS-INVESTMENT-POLICY-ENGLISH.pdf. [44]

ECOWAS-UEMOA (2022), *Guide méthodologique d'évaluation régionale des dépenses fiscales en Afrique de l'Ouest*, ECOWAS, UEMOA, Programme d'Appui à la Transition Fiscale (PATF), https://www.patf-ao.org/wp-content/uploads/2022/07/GUIDE-METHODOLOGIQUE-DEVALUATION-DES-DEPENSES-FISCALES-EN-AFRIQUE-DE-LOUEST_VERSION-DU-28-Juillet-2022.pdf (accessed on 5 March 2023). [39]

Gaspar, V., L. Jaramillo and P. Wingender (2016), "Tax Capacity and Growth: Is there a Tipping Point?", *IMF Working Papers*, No. 234, IMF, Washington, DC, https://www.imf.org/en/Publications/WP/Issues/2016/12/31/Tax-Capacity-and-Growth-Is-there-a-Tipping-Point-44436 (accessed on 19 April 2023). [17]

Ghrara, S. and B. El Morchid (2022), "Congés fiscaux et afflux des IDE dans les pays de la CEDEAO : Une application à l'aide de l'approche PMG", *International Journal of Accounting, Finance, Auditing, Management and Economics*, Vol. 3/4-1, pp. 21-42, https://doi.org/10.5281/ZENODO.6612018. [8]

House, C. and M. Shapiro (2008), "Temporary Investment Tax Incentives: Theory with Evidence from Bonus Depreciation", *American Economic Review*, Vol. 98/3, pp. 737-768, https://doi.org/10.1257/aer.98.3.737. [22]

IGF-OECD (2018), *Tax Incentives in Mining: Minimising risks to revenue*, Intergovernmental Forum on Mining, Minerals, Metals and Sustainable Development (IGF) and OECD, https://www.oecd.org/tax/beps/tax-incentives-in-mining-minimising-risks-to-revenue-oecd-igf.pdf (accessed on 8 March 2023). [32]

IMF (2021), "West African Economic and Monetary Union: Staff Report on Common Policies for Member Countries-Press Release; Staff Report; and Statement by the Executive Director for the West African Economic and Monetary Union", *Country Report*, No. 2021/049, IMF, Washington, DC, https://www.imf.org/en/Publications/CR/Issues/2021/03/02/West-African-Economic-and-Monetary-Union-Staff-Report-on-Common-Policies-for-Member-50139 (accessed on 5 March 2023). [40]

IMF, OECD, UN, World Bank (2015), *Options for Low Income Countries' Effective and Efficient Use of Ta Incentives for Investment, A report to the G-20 Development Working Group*, http://Options for Low Income Countries' Effective and Efficient. [24]

IMF-OECD (2017), *Tax Certainty: IMF/OECD Report for the G20 Finance Ministers*, IMF and OECD, https://www.oecd.org/tax/tax-policy/tax-certainty-report-oecd-imf-report-g20-finance-ministers-march-2017.pdf. [11]

IMF-OECD-UN-World Bank (2015), *Options for Low Income Countries' Effective and Efficient Use of Tax Incentives for Investment*, A report prepared for the G-20 Development Working Group by the IMF, OECD, UN and World Bank., https://www.oecd.org/tax/options-for-low-income-countries-effective-and-efficient-use-of-tax-incentives-for-investment.htm. [12]

James, S. (2014), *Tax and Non-Tax Incentives and Investments: Evidence and Policy Implications*, World Bank, Washington DC, https://papers.ssrn.com/sol3/papers.cfm?abstract_id=2401905. [6]

Keen, M. and M. Mansour (2009), "Revenue Mobilization in Sub-Saharan Africa: Challenges from Globalization", *IMF Working Papers*, No. 157, IMF, Washington, DC, https://www.imf.org/external/pubs/ft/wp/2009/wp09157.pdf (accessed on 17 March 2023). [14]

Klemm, A. (2009), "Causes, Benefits, and Risks of Business Tax Incentives", *IMF Working Paper*, No. 2009/021, IMF, Washington, DC, https://www.imf.org/en/Publications/WP/Issues/2016/12/31/Causes-Benefits-and-Risks-of-Business-Tax-Incentives-22628 (accessed on 1 March 2023). [35]

Klemm, A. and S. Van Parys (2012), "Empirical evidence on the effects of tax incentives", *International Tax and Public Finance*, Vol. 19/3, pp. 393-423, https://doi.org/10.1007/S10797-011-9194-8/METRICS. [4]

Lent, G. (1967), "Tax Incentives for Investment in Developing Countries", *IMF Staff Papers*, Vol. 1967/002, https://doi.org/10.5089/9781451947250.024.A003. [29]

Morisset, J. and N. Pirnia (1999), "How Tax Policy and Incentives Affect Foreign Direct Investment: A Review", *Foreign Investment Advisory Service*, World Bank, Washington, D.C., https://papers.ssrn.com/sol3/papers.cfm?abstract_id=632579 (accessed on 9 March 2023). [27]

OECD (2023), *Global Revenue Statistics Database*, https://stats.oecd.org/Index.aspx?DataSetCode=RS_GBL. [18]

OECD (2022), *FDI Qualities Indicators 2022*, https://www.oecd.org/investment/investment-policy/OECD-FDI-Qualities-Indicators-2022-update.pdf. [45]

OECD (2022), *FDI Qualities Policy Toolkit*, OECD Publishing, Paris, https://doi.org/10.1787/7ba74100-en. [25]

OECD (2022), *FDI Qualities Policy Toolkit*, OECD Publishing, Paris, https://doi.org/10.1787/7ba74100-en. [46]

OECD (2022), *OECD Investment Tax Incentives Database – 2022 Update: Tax incentives for sustainable development (brochure)*, OECD, Paris, http://www.oecd.org/investment/investment-policy/oecdinvestment-tax-incentives-database-2022-update-brochure.pdf (accessed on 14 March 2023). [2]

OECD (2022), *Tax Incentives and the Global Minimum Corporate Tax: Reconsidering Tax Incentives after the GloBE Rules*, OECD Publishing, Paris, https://doi.org/10.1787/25d30b96-en. [21]

OECD (2015), *Policy Framework for Investment, 2015 Edition*, OECD Publishing, Paris, https://doi.org/10.1787/9789264208667-en. [41]

OECD/ATAF/AUC (2022), *Revenue Statistics in Africa 2022*, OECD Publishing, Paris, https://doi.org/10.1787/ea66fbde-en-fr. [16]

PwC (2020), *Paying Taxes 2020: data explorer*, Paying Taxes 2020, https://www.pwc.com/gx/en/services/tax/publications/paying-taxes-2020/explorer-tool.html (accessed on 5 March 2023). [5]

Redonda, A., C. Von Haldenwang and F. Aliu (2021), “Tax Expenditure Reporting and Domestic Revenue Mobilization in Africa”, in Mosquera Valderrama, I., D. Lesage and W. Lips (eds.), *Taxation, International Cooperation and the 2030 Sustainable Development Agenda*, Springer, https://doi.org/10.1007/978-3-030-64857-2_9. [34]

Redonda, A., C. von Haldenwang and F. Aliu (2022), *Global Tax Expenditures Database [data set], Version 1.1.4*. [19]

Reuters (2020), “Namibia to repeal two tax policies, partly to appease EU”, *Reuters*, http://Namibia to repeal two tax policies, partly to appease EU (accessed on 19 April 2023). [36]

SADC (2023), *Tax Cooperation*, Southern African Development Community, https://www.sadc.int/pillars/tax-cooperation (accessed on 19 April 2023). [38]

Tax Foundation (2022), *Corporate Tax Rates around the World, 2022*, https://taxfoundation.org/data/all/global/corporate-tax-rates-by-country-2022/. [43]

UN-CIAT (2018), *Design and Assessment of Tax Incentives in Developing Countries: Selected Issues and a Country Experience*, United Nations, Inter-American Center of Tax Administrations, https://www.un.org/esa/ffd/wp-content/uploads/2018/02/tax-incentives_eng.pdf (accessed on 9 March 2023). [26]

UNIDO (2013), *Africa Investor Survey*, United Nations Industrial Development Organization. [10]

US Department of the Treasury (2010), *The Case for Temporary 100 Percent Expensing: Encouraging Business to Expand Now By Lowering the Cost of Investment*, US Department of the Treasury Office of Tax Policy, Washington, DC, https://home.treasury.gov/system/files/131/Report-Temporary-100percent-Expensing-2010.pdf (accessed on 1 March 2023). [31]

USAID (2004), *Effectiveness and Economic Impact of Tax Incentives in the SADC Region*, USAID, Report commissioned by SADC Tax Subcommittee, https://pdf.usaid.gov/pdf_docs/Pnacy929.pdf (accessed on 8 March 2023). [9]

Van Parys, S. and S. James (2010), "The effectiveness of tax incentives in attracting investment: panel data evidence from the CFA Franc zone", *International Tax and Public Finance*, Vol. 17/4, pp. 400-429, https://doi.org/10.1007/s10797-010-9140-1. [3]

Wen, J. (2020), *IMF Fiscal Affairs Special Series on COVID-19: Temporary Investment Incentives*, IMF, Washington, DC, https://www.imf.org/en/Publications/SPROLLs/covid19-special-notes (accessed on 1 March 2023). [30]

Zee, H., J. Stotsky and E. Ley (2002), "Tax Incentives for Business Investment: A Primer for Policy Makers in Developing Countries", *World Development*, Vol. 30/9, pp. 1497-1516, https://doi.org/10.1016/S0305-750X(02)00050-5. [20]

Notes

[1] Forward-looking corporate effective tax rates (ETRs) are a way of measuring the extent to which tax incentives affect tax costs and influence business investment and location decisions. Forward-looking ETRs are a useful indicator to compare the impact of tax incentives on effective taxation. The composite Effective Average Tax Rate (EATR) is constructed as a weighted average across finance- and asset-specific EATRs. It is a synthetic tax policy indicator reflecting the average tax contribution a firm makes on an investment project earning above-zero economic profits over its lifetime. The EATR is a useful indicator to compare the generosity of distinct types of preferential tax treatment relative to the standard tax treatment and to assess tax relief from investing in one as opposed to another sector, region or country or to assess the relief provided through specific incentive designs everything else being equal.

[2] Data from the Global Tax Expenditures Database (GTED) and OECD revenue statistics. In Eswatini, Madagascar, Seychelles and DRC taxes incentives on goods and services (including VAT, customs duties and excise tax) cost up to double in terms of revenue forgone than CIT incentives (Redonda, von Haldenwang and Aliu, 2022[19]). This shows the importance of looking at the full scope of tax benefits available to investors in considering both the costs of incentives and their policy goals, and would merit further research and analysis. The GTED data covers 18 jurisdictions in Africa, 12 jurisdictions in Asia-Pacific, 33 jurisdictions in Europe and North America and 14 jurisdictions in the LAC region. OECD Revenue Statistics cover 29 jurisdictions in Africa, 23 in Asia-Pacific, 32 in Europe and North America and 26 jurisdictions in LAC.

[3] This tax allowance in South Africa was introduced in the Income Tax Act, Section 12I, and got repealed in March 2020.

[4] This tax allowance in South Africa was introduced in the Income Tax Act, Section 12I, and got repealed in March 2020.

Annex A. Additional details on classifications

The ITID considers policy area being targeted by evaluating whether a specific design or eligibility condition of the tax incentive relates to one of six policy goals (Table 1). The policy areas identified in the ITID build on those identified in the OECD FDI Qualities Indicators (OECD, 2022[45]) and the FDI Qualities policy toolkit (OECD, 2022[46]).

Table 1. Targeting sustainable development through eligibility conditions and design dimensions of investment tax incentives

Column 1 lists policy areas identified in the ITID. The table identifies how economies target these respective clusters, either through eligibility conditions or the design features of tax incentives (columns 2-5).

(1) Sustainable Development Areas	(2) Outcome condition	(3) Sector condition	(4) Preferential treatment for certain qualifying income	(5) Preferential treatment for certain qualifying expenditure
Employment & job creation	(a) Create a minimum number of new jobs;			(a) Wages of newly created jobs; (b) Wages of recent graduates; (c) Wages of employees, including for women or workers with disabilities.
Environmental impact	(a) Ensure some or a certain level of energy efficiency improvement.	(a) Electricity generation from renewable energy sources;[1] (b) Waste management.		(a) Acquisition of machinery for electricity production from renewable energy sources; (b) Improving the energy performance of machinery or buildings (e.g. via building retrofitting).
Job quality and skills	(a) Reach a minimum level of expenditure on training and education; (b) Pay an average wage at a certain level.			(a) Expenditure on training and education of employees; (b) Wages of trainees and apprentices; (c) Training expenditures for women re-entering the workforce or workers

				with disabilities; (d) Expenditures related to building training facilities.
Local linkages	(a) Source a minimum share of inputs from the local market; (b) Source a minimum share of inputs from local SMEs.			(a) Expenditures on inputs sourced from SMEs.
Promoting Exports	(a) Achieve a minimum export share in sales.		(a) Income from exports; (b) Income from transit trade.	(a) Export promotion expenditure.[2]
Social Inclusion	(a) Employ a minimum share of female workers; (b) Employ a minimum share of workers with disabilities; (c) Founding members of a company must be people with disabilities.			(a) Wages of female workers or workers with disabilities; (b) Training expenditures for women re-entering the workforce or workers with disabilities.

Notes: Eligibility conditions and design features listed in the table are used by at least one economy included in the database. The list may evolve in the future when economy coverage extends.

[1] Includes only tax incentives benefiting electricity generation from renewable energy sources, but not electricity generation from non-renewable sources. Tax incentive may be part of a broader special regime that benefits other sector of the economy.

[2] Refers to expenses incurred for the purpose of seeking opportunities and promoting the export of goods or services produced in the economy (e.g. publicity and advertisements abroad, export market research, participation in trade fairs amongst others).

Other policy goals commonly targeted with tax incentives relate to infrastructure and innovation. Infrastructure can relate to a broad set of areas, including transport, utilities (e.g. electricity or gas distribution, water and sewage disposal structures), construction or ICT. CIT incentives promoting innovation commonly target R&D-related costs (e.g. wages of R&D employees, current costs of R&D projects, assets) or income (e.g. income from R&D or registered patents).

5 Promoting investment for green growth

This chapter discusses the specific enabling conditions for green investment in SADC, including key elements of the broader framework for environmental protection, and targeted financial, technical and information support to attract and facilitate green FDI.

Investment for green growth is central to the SADC Regional Indicative Strategic Development Plan 2020-30 and needs to be scaled-up significantly to advance sustainable development in Southern Africa, and achieve national economic, social and environmental policy goals. Green growth means fostering growth and development while preserving natural assets and ensuring that they continue to provide the resources and environmental services on which our well-being relies. Beyond mainstreaming green growth considerations into investments in general, so as to minimise their environmental footprint, this requires investments in new technologies, services and infrastructure that make more sustainable claims on natural resources (green investments). Under certain circumstances, foreign direct investment (FDI) can contribute the needed financial and technological resources to deliver green growth. But foreign investors can also deteriorate environmental outcomes and hamper sustainable development. This chapter discusses the specific enabling conditions for green investment in SADC and targeted policies designed to attract and facilitate green FDI.

Green growth and climate change in Southern Africa

The Southern African Development Community's (SADC) path to green growth faces both challenges and opportunities. Challenges include a heavy dependence on natural resources and unsustainable use of these resulting in degradation of land and water, a major investment gap for basic infrastructure and increasing vulnerability to climate change and extreme weather. Addressing these challenges also presents an opportunity for SADC to promote green investment. The imperative to urgently scale up access to electricity and promote energy security, the region's high renewable energy potential and the need to improve the efficiency of how natural resources are used illustrate the potential for green investment in Southern Africa. A measured and inclusive approach, based on a sound policy framework that promotes investment in green sectors and facilitates the greening of investment overall, can help address challenges and promote sustainable development in SADC.

Natural resources are critical for continued development in Southern Africa

Southern African countries are at different stages of development, but almost all their economies, have grown by over 50%, and six have more than doubled since 2000 (Table 5.1). SADC countries have relied heavily on natural resources to support economic development in past decades, and primary sectors continue to contribute substantially, despite the rising importance of industry and services across the region. In 2020, rents from natural resource amounted to over 10% of GDP in Angola, DRC, Mozambique and Zambia, while agriculture, forestry and fishing made up over 20% of GDP in Comoros, Tanzania, Mozambique, Madagascar, Malawi and DRC (World Bank, 2023[1]). Due to illegal logging and export of timber, in some SADC countries the impact of forestry and fishing on the economy is likely to be underestimated in national statistics (Browne, Kelly and Pilgrim, 2022[2]).

Heavy reliance on natural resources for development, coupled with unstainable use of these resources, means that the environment costs of growth have been high. Since 1990, Southern Africa has experienced the highest rate of deforestation in Africa, contributing 31% to Africa's deforested area. Forest cover in the region has shrunk by 15% over the last 30 years, compared to a 4% decrease in non-OECD countries and a 2% increase in forest cover in the OECD (Figure 5.1). The largest decrease in forest cover is observed in Malawi (-36%), Comoros (-29%), and Tanzania (-20%), while forest cover has increased slightly in Eswatini (8%). In Madagascar, more than 80% of the original forest cover has been lost, with primary forests covering only 12% of the country at present (SBDC, 2014[3]). Deforestation has also been a major driver of carbon emissions in the region. Southern Africa still generates only 1% of global carbon emissions, and a quarter of Africa's emissions, yet emissions per unit of GDP are declining at a slower rate than other non-OECD economies, and have risen in six SADC countries (Figure 5.2).

Table 5.1. Selected economic and environmental indicators

MS	GDP growth over 2000-20 (%)	Agriculture, forestry & fishing (% of GDP)	Natural resource rents (% of GDP)	Poverty rate (% of population)	2022 EPI Rank
AGO	164%	9.1	25.5	32.3	151
BWA	94%	2.2	0.7	19.3	35
COD	191%	20.9	14.9	63.9	85
COM	73%	35.8	1.5	42.4	119
LSO	53%	4.8	5.1	49.7	141
MDG	66%	24.7	5.3	70.7	167
MOZ	252%	26.2	11.7	46.1	144
MUS	83%	3.1	0.0	10.3	77
MWI	136%	22.7	4.0	50.7	97
NAM	89%	9.2	2.0	17.4	44
SWZ	88%	8.1	3.9	58.9	75
SYC	82%	2.1	0.2	25.3	32
TZA	247%	26.7	3.9	26.4	134
ZAF	59%	2.5	3.9	55.5	116
ZMB	204%	3.0	11.8	54.4	69
ZWE	4%	8.8	6.8	38.3	106

Note: GDP data refer to 2021; value added shares and natural resource rents to 2020; and poverty rates range from 2016-21 depending on survey year. EPI = Environmental Performance Index.
Source: Authors' elaboration based on World Bank (2023[1]); UNDP-OPHI (2022[4]); and Wolf et al. (2022[5]).

Figure 5.1. Forest cover as a share of land area in SADC, 1990-2020

Percentage of total land area (%)

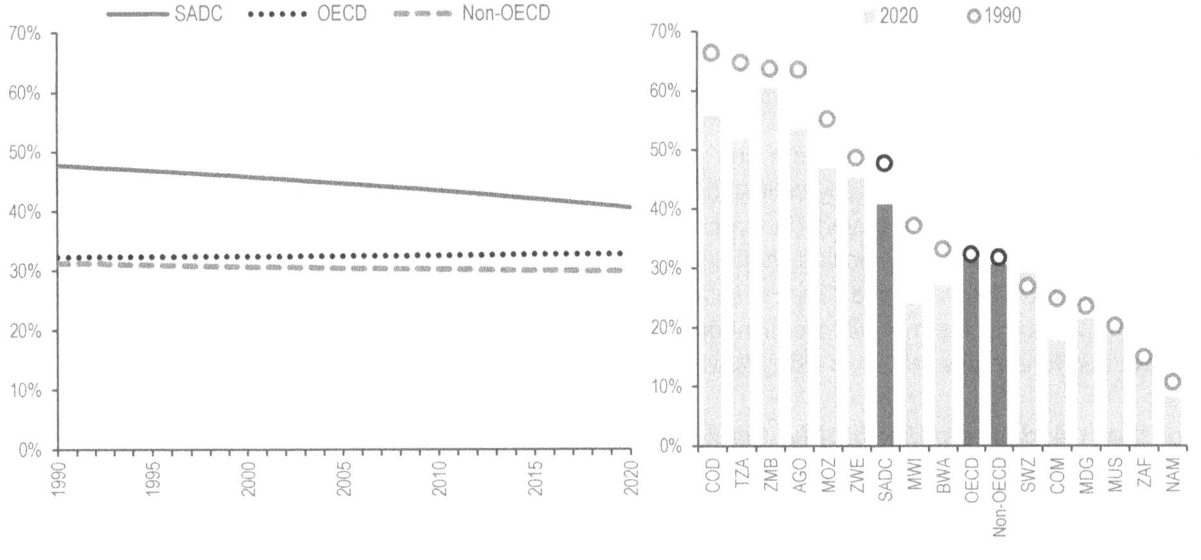

Source: FAOStat, Agri-environmental indicators – Land use, http://www.fao.org/faostat/, accessed 6.02.23.

Figure 5.2. Carbon emissions in Southern Africa, 1990-2020

CO_2 / GDP (kgCO_2 per 2015 US$)

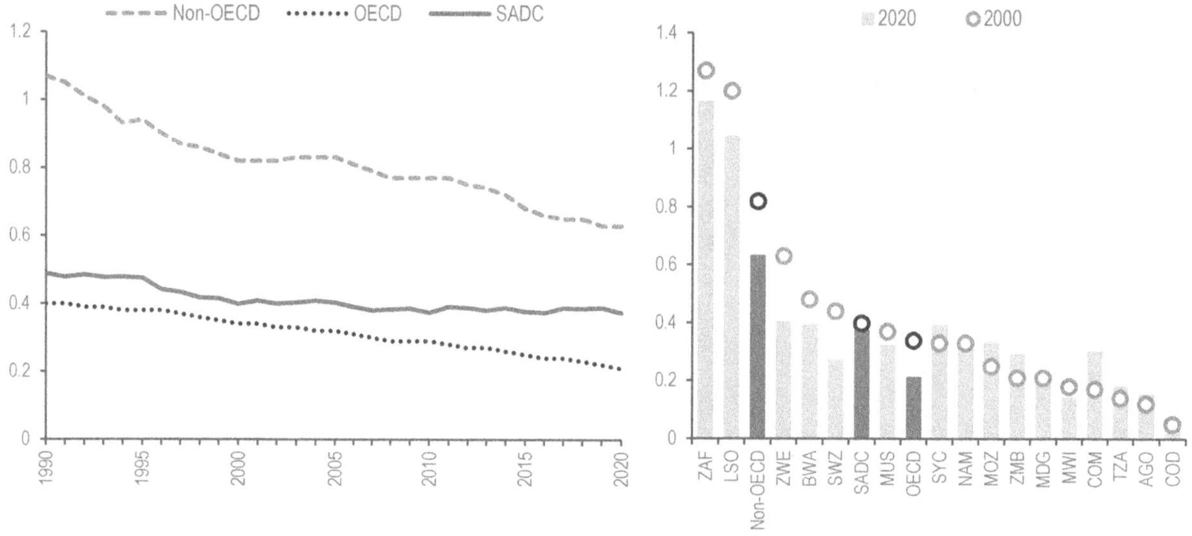

Source: Authors' elaboration based on IEA Greenhouse Gas Emissions from Energy database (2022[6]).

Urbanisation has exacerbated land degradation and biodiversity loss and brought additional environmental challenges. According to the 2022 Environmental Performance Index that covers 180 countries worldwide, most SADC countries rank poorly in terms of progress toward improving environmental health, protecting ecosystems, and mitigating climate change, with eight countries ranking among the lowest 50 scores. Greater vehicle ownership, burning of agricultural and other waste and construction activities have increased air pollution in urban areas, and mining activities accompanied by the discharge of untreated wastewater and solid waste into water bodies is impacting water quality in rivers and lakes. According to some estimates, an estimated 50% of South Africa's wetlands have been destroyed and 82% of its main river ecosystems are threatened.

Southern Africa's land, forests, rivers and coasts support employment and livelihoods for most of the region's people and are especially critical for continued progress on reducing poverty. Over a third of the population lives in extreme poverty in ten countries in the region (UNDP-OPHI, 2022[4]). The number of people living in poverty is particularly high in remote rural areas where peoples' livelihoods rely on small-scale agriculture, fisheries and forest resources. Escalating deforestation, soil degradation, biodiversity loss and over-exploitation of wild-life, fisheries and rangelands undermine the development prospects for present and future generations in many SADC countries.

Southern Africa remains highly vulnerable to climate change

The developmental challenges facing SADC countries, exacerbated by poor economic and political governance, make the region highly susceptible to the effects of climate change. The 16 SADC states have recorded 37% of all weather-related disasters in Africa in the past four decades. These affected 228 million people, left 2.7 million homeless and inflicted damage in excess of US$ 26 billion (ISS, 2021[7]; CRED, 2023[8]). Climate change is expected to increase the frequency and intensity of extreme hazards such as floods, droughts, storms and wildfires, damaging infrastructure, destroying agricultural crops, disrupting livelihoods and causing loss of lives. Many communities in the region have little ability to adapt, and their dependency on natural resources and exposure to repeated and extreme hazards render them extremely vulnerable.

The Notre Dame-Global Adaptation Index (ND-GAIN) measures the predisposition of countries to be negatively impacted by climate-related hazards across life-supporting sectors, like water, food, health, and infrastructure (i.e. vulnerability), against their economic, social and governance ability to make effective use of investments for adaptation actions thanks to a safe and efficient business environment (i.e. readiness). The index suggests that the majority of SADC countries exhibit high levels of vulnerability combined with low levels of readiness, with the Democratic Republic of Congo (DRC), Zimbabwe and Madagascar among the least resilient (Figure 5.3). Seychelles, Namibia and Botswana are somewhat more resilient with high levels of vulnerability paired with high readiness, while South Africa is relatively less vulnerable but also less ready. With moderate levels of vulnerability and significantly higher levels of readiness, Mauritius is the only SADC country considered to be resilient to the effects of climate change.

Figure 5.3. Resilience to climate change in SADC

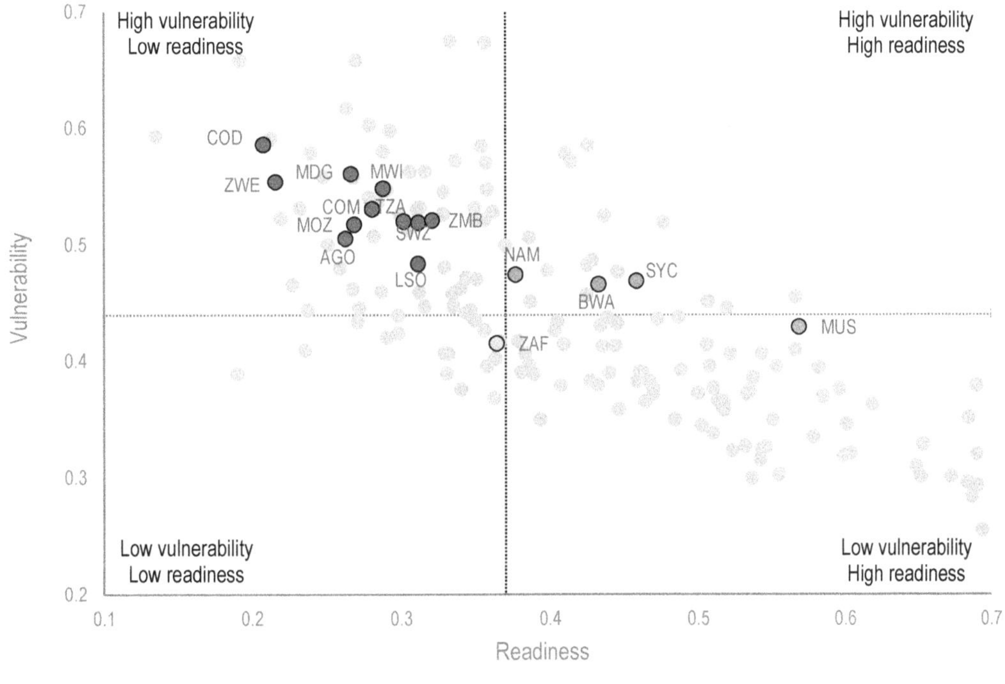

Source: Authors' elaboration based on ND-GAIN Index (2022[9]).

FDI can improve access to clean and affordable energy in the region

The SADC region faces a huge power deficit due to lack of investment in the power sector. Russia's invasion of Ukraine has sent food, energy and other commodity prices soaring, increasing the strains on SADC economies already hard hit by the COVID-19 pandemic. The overlapping crises are affecting many parts of SADC's energy systems, including reversing positive trends in improving access to modern energy, with 4% more people living without electricity in 2021 than in 2019. Over 80% of the electricity is generated from coal, and the energy sector is responsible for 65% of CO_2 emissions in the region (IEA, 2022[10]). A disruption to power supplies is a major threat to sustainable development in the region.

Accelerating investment in clean energy is critical to urgently scale up access to electricity, and at the same time mitigate climate change. Private investment, and in particular FDI, can play a key role in advancing the energy transition and supporting rural electrification. Thanks to their financial and technical advantages, multinational enterprises (MNEs) are key players in the deployment of capital- and R&D-intensive clean energy technologies across borders, accounting for 30% of global new investments in renewable energy (OECD, 2022[11]).

In Southern Africa, new (or greenfield) FDI projects in renewable energy have been rising steadily over the last two decades, although the value of these investments remains small in comparison to greenfield FDI stocks in fossil fuels, which still account for 78% of energy FDI stocks in the region (Figure 5.4). Nevertheless, since 2018, FDI flows to renewables have surpassed FDI flows to fossil fuels, both in volume and value, showing promising signs in terms of FDI's growing contribution to the energy transition. The variation across countries remains wide. In Angola and Mozambique, fossil fuels account for 78% and 45% of total greenfield FDI accumulated since 2003, and over 94% of FDI stocks in the energy sector. In Tanzania, Malawi, and Botswana, fossil fuels account for over a quarter of overall greenfield FDI stocks and also dwarf renewable energy FDI. Madagascar, Zimbabwe and DRC also lag behind in terms of attracting renewable energy FDI. Conversely, in Namibia, Seychelles, Lesotho and Eswatini, renewable energy FDI dominates the energy sector and has attracted a sizeable share of greenfield FDI, ranging from 10% in Eswatini to 32% in Namibia. In Zambia and South Africa, the gap between renewable and conventional energy in terms of FDI attraction is smaller, but there is a clear trend toward greener energy.

Figure 5.4. FDI in renewable energy is rising

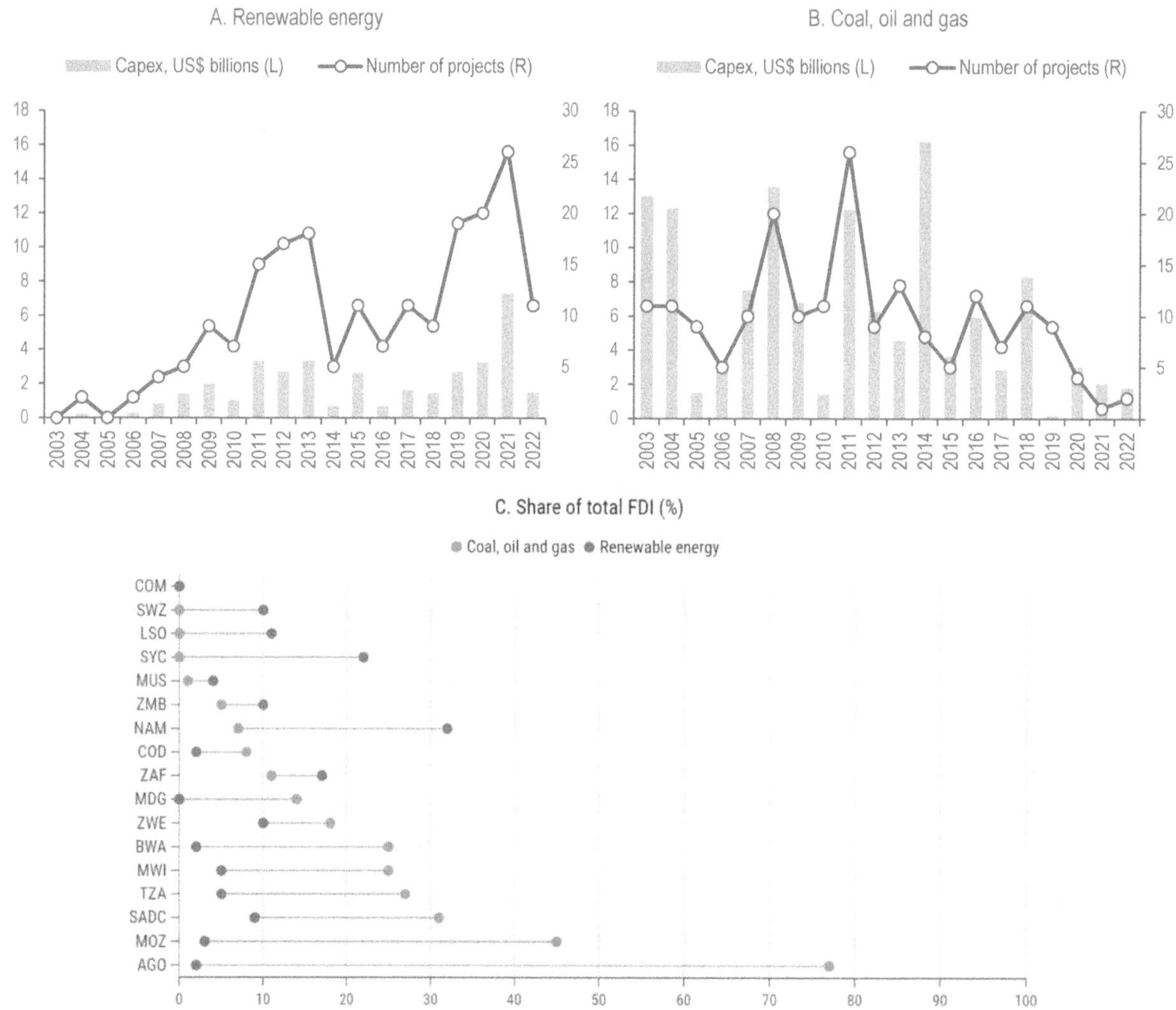

Note: Figure C is calculated using greenfield FDI flows accumulated over 2003-22.
Source: OECD based on Financial Times FDI Markets (2022[12])

Policy framework for green growth and climate change

Strong government commitment to combat climate change and to support low-carbon growth, underpinned by a coherent policy framework and clear decarbonisation targets, provides investors with encouraging signals regarding the government's climate ambitions. Setting a clear, long-term transition trajectory that is linked to the national vision or goals for growth and development is critically important to build capacity for investors to understand transition risks, and to attracting foreign investment that contributes to the country's climate agenda.

SADC's international commitments to green growth

SADC recognises the importance of sustainable use and management of the environment in the fight against poverty and food insecurity. SADC Member States have committed themselves to integrated and sustainable development, and climate change adaptation and mitigation. This commitment is reflected by the SADC Treaty establishing the organisation, and active participation in the negotiations and ratification of major Multilateral Environmental Agreements (MEAs). All SADC Member States have ratified the three Rio Conventions: the Convention on Biological Diversity, the United Nations Convention to Combat Desertification (UNCCD), and the United Nations Framework Convention on Climate Change (UNFCCC). There is, however, currently a lack of cohesive regional target-setting across all three Rio Conventions within SADC. These targets are often expressed differently between countries, while the level of detail varies in terms of commitments and implementation plans.

In addition to the Rio Conventions, SADC members have ratified or acceded to most major global MEAs on biodiversity, climate and atmosphere, land and water resources, and chemicals and waste, though some exceptions remain (Table 5.2). Four countries in the region are neither parties to the Convention on Migratory Species nor the Agreement on the Conservation of African-Eurasian Migratory Waterbirds (AEWA), and only three have ratified the Lusaka Agreement on Co-operative Enforcement Operations Directed at Illegal Trade in Wild Fauna and Flora, suggesting that more progress can be made in terms of protecting biodiversity. Three countries have yet to accede to the Rotterdam Convention on prior informed consent for hazardous materials and pesticides (Angola, Comoros and Seychelles), and four countries to the Minamata convention on Mercury (Angola, DRC, Malawi, Mozambique), while less than half of SADC countries are parties to the Bamako Convention remaining potentially vulnerable to illegal dumping of spent chemicals, hazardous wastes and banned pesticides. Only two countries (Namibia and South Africa) have ratified the UN Watercourses Convention, although all mainland SADC countries are party to the SADC Protocol on Shared Watercourse (discussed in greater detail below).

As of 2018, all SADC Members signed and ratified the Paris Agreement under the UNFCCC and submitted their Nationally Determined Contributions (NDCs) to the convention, joining the global collaborative effort to mitigate and adapt to climate change. All SADC members have committed to reducing their GHG emissions, albeit to varying degrees, and all but three countries in the region have submitted updated NDCs, in line with the five-year cycle mandated by the Paris Agreement. These updated NDCs have universally provided additional information for clarity, transparency and understanding. Twelve SADC countries strengthened the adaptation component in their revised NDCs, and 11 have strengthened or added policies and actions. Only nine revised NDCs have strengthened or added sectoral targets while only five have reduced the total emissions target for 2030.

Collectively SADC NDCs are not yet aligned with the objectives of the Paris Agreement of limiting the increase in global average temperature to well below 2°C. Only five countries in the region have committed to achieving net-zero GHG emissions by 2050, including Comoros which has already achieved net-zero (Table 5.3). Emissions reduction targets are specified in ways that are not directly comparable across countries, due to different time frames and business-as-usual scenarios. Eight countries have both an unconditional target, and a significantly more ambitious conditional target, and six countries only commit to emissions reductions conditional on international support. The conditions of these targets differ across countries, but frequently include access to international aid in the form of financial resources, technology transfer and capacity building. Five countries in the region do not specify any sectoral targets for emissions reductions.

South Africa is the only country to have submitted a long-term strategy document in addition to its NDC. Ambitious long-term strategies are vital since current near-term NDCs are only sufficient enough to limit warming to 2.7-3.7°C. Moreover, long-term strategies provide a pathway to a whole-of-society transformation and a vital link between shorter-term NDCs and the long-term objectives of the Paris Agreement. Given the 30-year time horizon, these strategies offer many other benefits, including guiding countries to avoid costly investments in high-emissions technologies, supporting just and equitable transitions, promoting technological innovation, planning for new sustainable infrastructure in light of future climate risks, and sending early and predictable signals to investors about envisaged long-term societal changes.

Table 5.2. Multilateral environmental agreements (MEAs) ratified by SADC Member States

Year of ratification / accession

MEA	AGO	BWA	COD	COM	LSO	MDG	MOZ	MUS	MWI	NAM	SWZ	SYC	TZA	ZAF	ZMB	ZWE
Biological diversity																
AEWA		2017				2007		2001	2019		2013		1999	2002		2012
Cartagena Protocol	2009	2003	2005	2009	2003	2004	2003	2003	2009	2005	2006	2004	2003	2003	2004	2005
Convention on Biodiversity	1998	1996	1995	1994	1995	1996	1995	1993	1994	1997	1995	1993	1996	1996	1993	1995
CITES	2013	1978	1976	1995	2003	1975	1981	1975	1982	1991	1997	1977	1980	1975	1981	1981
Convention on Migratory Species	2007		1990			2007	2009	2004	2019		2013	2005	1999	1992		2012
Lusaka Convention					1995									1996	1995	
Nagoya Protocol	2017	2014	2015	2014	2015	2014	2014	2014	2014	2014	2016	2014	2018	2014	2016	2017
Chemicals and waste																
Basel Convention	2017	1998	1995	1995	2000	1999	1997	1993	1994	1995	2005	1993	1993	1994	1995	2012
Bamako Convention	2016		1998	2004			1999						1993			1992
Minamata Convention		2017		2019	2017	2017		2017		2017	2017	2017	2021	2019	2017	2021
Rotterdam Convention		2008	2005		2008	2004	2010	2005	2009	2005	2012		2004	2004	2011	2012
Stockholm Convention	2007	2004	2005	2007	2004	2006	2006	2004	2009	2005	2006	2008	2004	2004	2006	2012
Climate and atmosphere																
Kyoto Protocol	2007	2005	2005	2008	2005	2005	2005	2005	2005	2005	2006	2005	2005	2005	2006	2009
Montreal Protocol	2000	1992	1995	1995	1994	1997	2994	1992	1991	1993	1993	1993	1993	1990	1990	1993
Paris Agreement	2021	2017	2018	2017	2017	2016	2018	2016	2017	2016	2016	2016	2018	2016	2017	2017
UNFCCC	2000	1994	1995	1995	1995	1999	1995	1994	1994	1995	1997	1994	1996	1997	1994	1994
Vienna Convention	2000	1992	1995	1995	1994	1997	1994	1992	1991	1993	1993	1993	1993	1990	1990	1993
Land and water resources																
Ramsar Convention		1997	1996	1995	2004	1998	2004	2001	1997	1995	2013	2005	2000		1991	2013
UNCCD	1997	1996	1997	1998	1996	1997	1997	1996	1996	1997	1996	1997	1997	1997	1996	1997
UN Watercourses Convention										2014				2014		
UN Convention on the Law of the Sea	1994	1994	1994	1994	2007	2001	1997	1994	2010	1994	2012	1994	1994	1998	1994	1994

Source: Authors' elaboration based on https://www.informea.org/en.

Table 5.3. NDC targets of SADC Members

GHG reduction relative to Business-As-Usual (BAU) levels

MS	Unconditional target	Conditional target	Net-Zero Target	LTS	Sector Targets
AGO	15% by 2025	25% by 2025	None.	None	Energy, AFOLU, Industry, Waste
BWA	15% by 2030	None	None.	None	None
COD	2% by 2030	19% by 2030	None.	None	Energy, AFOLU, Waste
COM	1.15% by 2030	23% by 2030	Achieved	None	Energy, FOLU, Waste
LSO	10% by 2030	35% by 2030	None.	None	Energy
MDG	None	14% by 2030	None.	None	None
MOZ	None	40 MtCO2eq between 2020 and 2025	None.	None	FOLU
MUS	14% by 2030	40% by 2030	2070	None	Energy, Transport, Waste, IPPU, AFOLU
MWI	6% by 2040	51% by 2040	2050	None	Energy, IPPU, Waste, Agriculture
NAM	9% by 2040	91% by 2040	2050	None	Energy, IPPU & RAC, AFOLU, Waste
SWZ	5% by 2030	14% by 2030	None.	None	Energy, Waste, Industry, AFOLU
SYC	None	73.7% by 2030	2050	None	Energy, RAC, transport, waste
TZA	None	30-35% by 2030	None.	None	None
ZAF	to 350-420 MtCO2e by 2030	None	2050	Yes	None
ZMB	None	25-47% by 2030	None	None	None
ZWE	None	40% by 2030	None	None	Energy/transport, IPPU, AFOLU, Waste

Note: Details on the conditions of the targets can be found in the source. BAU scenarios and base years vary by country. IPPU = Industrial Processes and Product Use; AFOLU = Agriculture, Forestry and Other Land Use; RAC = Refrigeration and Air Conditioning.
Source: NDCs were retrieved from the official registry (https://www4.unfccc.int/sites/ndcstaging/Pages/Home.aspx).

Regional environmental co-operation

Several legal instruments for regional co-operation and integration in environment and climate change have been developed in SADC. These include the Protocol on Environmental Management for Sustainable Development (2014); the Protocol on Forestry (2002); the Protocol on Fisheries (2001); the Revised Protocol on Shared Watercourse Systems (2000); the Protocol on Wildlife Conservation and Law Enforcement (1999); and Protocol on Development of Tourism (1998).

The overall objectives of the Protocol on Environmental Management for Sustainable Development are to promote sustainable use and transboundary management of the environment and natural resources, and to harmonise all existing regional instruments that deal with environmental issues. The Protocol covers environmental issues such as climate change, waste and chemicals, biodiversity, land management, and water resources, as well as cross-cutting issues on gender, science, technology, trade and investment. A total of 14 SADC Member States have signed the Protocol and ratification is at various stages, with 11 Members required to operationalise the Protocol. Despite the fact that the Protocol is not yet in force, the region has made some strides in implementation of some of the targets. These include the development of the: Regional Climate Change Strategy, the Regional Green Economy Strategy and Action Plan for Sustainable Development and the Global Climate Change Alliance Plus in the SADC region.

The Revised Protocol on Shared Watercourse Systems in SADC (Revised Protocol) was the first binding agreement amongst SADC member states, illustrating the important role water plays within the region. The Revised Protocol stresses the importance of taking a basin-wide approach to water management rather than that of territorial sovereignty. It outlines specific objectives including improving co-operation to promote sustainable and co-ordinated management, protection and use of transboundary watercourses, and promoting the SADC Agenda of Regional Integration and Poverty Alleviation. The Revised Protocol allows countries to enter into specific basin-wide agreements, which is the approach promoted under the UN Watercourses Convention. For instance, the governments of Botswana, Lesotho, Namibia and South Africa formalised the Orange-Senqu River Commission (ORASECOM) following the regional ratification of the Revised Protocol.

Southern Africa is bestowed with forest resources covering 41% of the region's total land area, which provide timber and non-timber forest products, domestic wood energy, and a habitat for wildlife. Forests are also important for soil protection, water conservation, food, and climate change mitigation through carbon sequestration. The 2002 Protocol on Forestry provides a policy framework for sustainable forest management in the SADC region. Objectives addressed in this protocol include increasing public awareness of forestry and capacity building. More specifically, the framework addresses research gaps, laws, education and training, the harmonisation of regional sustainable management practises, increasing efficiencies of utilisation and facilitation of trade, equitable use of local forests and a respect for traditional knowledge and uses.

The Protocol on Wildlife Conservation and Law Enforcement is an inter-state regulation affirming that member states have the sovereign right to manage their wildlife resources and the corresponding responsibility for sustainable use and conservation of these resources. The aim is to establish a common framework for the conservation and sustainable use of wildlife resources in the SADC region and to assist with the effective enforcement of laws governing those resources.

Policy framework for environmental protection

SADC countries have recognised the mutually reinforcing relationship between human rights and environmental rule of law. The constitutions of six SADC Members explicitly state the right to a healthy or balanced environment, while another eight contain clauses to ensure the protection of the environment and natural resources by the State and its citizens. Only the constitutions of Botswana and Mauritius omit these rights but have afforded them through a variety of laws, policies and visions.

SADC's Policy and Strategy for Environment and Sustainable Development (1996) called for a departure from fragmented sectoral approaches to environmental management and urged the region to pursue a unified strategy to achieve the consistent integration of environmental impact assessment (EIA) in decision-making. Since then, SADC Members made great strides in formalising EIA into their legal frameworks, with all SADC countries now having promulgated laws in this regard. Two countries in SADC, Lesotho and Mauritius, do not have any specific EIA regulations, but have detailed guidelines for the EIA process.

SADC Members have adopted the same general approach to EIA, which is mandated under an environmental agency (e.g. the Ministry of Environment) or the Vice-President's Office in the case of Tanzania. EIA processes consist of similar procedures in line with principles set out by the International Association for Impact Assessment (IAIA), involving screening, scoping, impact assessment, approval, and monitoring. The exceptions are Angola, the DRC, Namibia and Zimbabwe, which combined the screening and scoping phases into one, and Comoros, where the environmental law does not have a system in place for screening or pre-evaluation of small-scale projects and there is no mention of scoping or follow-up.

With few exceptions, laws and policies of SADC countries provide for the three critical procedural rights of access to information, public participation, and access to remedies, including grievance redress mechanisms and other project specific complaints processes (Table 5.4). These procedural rights are necessary to ensure that EIAs can effectively identify community concerns about development projects, and therefore critical for environmental governance. They also ensure that the human rights obligations to a clean and safe environment are protected.

Table 5.4. Common elements of EIA systems in SADC

	Year of Act / Regulation	Screening list	Public participation	Access to information	Access to justice	EMP & monitoring	SEA	Transboundary EIA	Certified consultants
AGO	1998 / 2020	■	◘	■	■	◘	□	□	□
BWA	2005 / 2012	■	■	◘	◘	■	■	◘	■
COD	2011 / 2014	■	◘	■	■	◘	■	□	□
COM	1995 / 2008	□	□	◘	◘	□	□	□	□
LSO	2008	■	◘	◘	■	◘	◘	□	□
MDG	1990 / 2004	■	◘	■	■	◘	◘	□	□
MOZ	1997 / 2015	■	■	■	■	◘	□	□	□
MUS	2002	■	◘	◘	◘	◘	◘	□	□
MWI	2017 / 2019	■	■	■	■	◘	◘	□	□
NAM	2007 / 2013	■	◘	■	■	◘	□	□	□
SWZ	2002 / 2000	■	■	■	■	◘	◘	◘	■
SYC	1994 / 1996	■	◘	◘	■	◘	□	□	◘
TZA	2004 / 2018	■	■	■	■	◘	◘	◘	■
ZAF	1998 / 2017	■	◘	■	■	◘	□	□	■
ZMB	2011 / 1997	■	■	■	■	◘	◘	■	□
ZWE	2002 / 2007	■	◘	■	◘	◘	□	□	□

Note: ■ = Clear legal requirement in EIA laws and regulations; ◘ = Partial legal requirement (e.g. no regulations or guidelines); □ = No legal requirement. SEA = Strategic Environmental Assessment; EMP = Environmental Management Plan.
Source: Authors based on national EIA legislation and Walmsley and Patel (2020[13]).

EIA processes are most effective where key interested and affected parties are consulted at an early stage of the process, and empowered to contribute to assessing alternatives, identifying community issues and concerns and ensuring that these are addressed in the EIA report. While some level of public consultation is required as part of the EIA process in almost all SADC countries, the timing and mode of consultation vary significantly. The scope of participation ranges from full engagement of interested and affected parties to various means, including public meetings and focus groups (e.g. in South Africa), to the passive placement of the EIA report for public review and comment (e.g. in Mauritius). It is generally considered best practice to consult the public as early in the EIA process as possible, that is, in the scoping phase. Eight SADC countries (Botswana, Lesotho, Malawi, Mozambique, Namibia, South Africa, Tanzania and Zambia) require this. Ten SADC countries require the proponent to undertake public participation during the preparation phase of the EIA. In Madagascar, Mauritius, and Seychelles, the authorities will hold public hearings as the sole means of public consultation, while in Comoros there are no regulations or guidelines on specific measures to be followed for public participation and consultation.

Lack of effective post-EIA follow-up and implementation of an Environmental Management Plan (EMP) reduces the value of the EIA process. In all SADC countries, the EIA must include measures setting out how the proponent proposes to avoid, reduce, manage or control the adverse impacts of the development on the environment in an EMP. In practice, the general standards of EMP formulation are often poor due to a lack of guidance. Compounding the situation is the general lack of post-EIA follow-up and compliance monitoring. Ten SADC countries make provisions for inspections, audits and monitoring by the authorities. In practice this is seldom achieved due to a range of factors including lack of public sector resources. Four countries (DRC, Eswatini, South Africa and Zambia) place the responsibility for project compliance monitoring and auditing on the proponent, who is required to submit regular monitoring and auditing reports to the authorities. This approach requires that the project proponent take ownership of the environmental monitoring process and the management of related risk. Only Botswana formally requires joint monitoring and auditing, with the proponent doing the day-to day compliance monitoring activities, and the authorities carrying out periodic inspections.

Strategic environmental assessment (SEA) continues to gain momentum, and much of the newer legislation requires SEAs for policies, plans and programmes, notably in ten SADC countries. South Africa has a long history of SEA practice dating back to the mid-1990s; however, this practice has been voluntary with no formal legal framework. With the exception of Botswana, DRC and South Africa, currently no regulations or guideline set out the procedures for the implementation of SEAs, leaving considerable room for interpretation. The legislation in Madagascar and Malawi does not refer to SEAs specifically, but both countries require an EIA of new national policies, plans and programmes. The Environmental Protection Act of Mauritius lists the activities that require a SEA, but no other mention is made in the main body of the act. The only reference to SEA is a definition in Seychelles, and no mention of SEAs is made in the environmental laws of Angola, Comoros, Mozambique, Namibia and Zimbabwe. In Namibia and Mozambique, several SEAs have nevertheless been carried out for a variety of sectors, including mining, agriculture, forestry development, and coastal zone planning.

The application of EIA principles to the assessment of transboundary impacts of investment remains limited in SADC, and only Zambia provides a framework for the control and restriction of any contaminants that may have a regional or global effect. In Botswana, Eswatini and Tanzania, environmental authorities are required to initiate a consultative process with the relevant authorities of countries that may be significantly adversely affected by a proposed activity. In Lesotho, the EIA report must include an indication of whether the environment of any other State is likely to be affected by the proposed project and what mitigation measures are to be undertaken, but there is no reference to consultation with the concerned countries. In Malawi, the EIA Guidelines mention transboundary assessment as one of the components to be included in the EIA report but there is no mention of it in the corresponding legislation. All other SADC countries do not require transboundary EIA in their environmental laws, but may be signatories to trans-boundary agreements which require sharing of information (e.g. Orange-Senqu River Commission, the SADC Protocol on Shared Watercourse Systems), as well as some trans-frontier conservation initiatives.

Ensuring a high level of professional quality and conduct of EIA practitioners is central to the effectiveness of the EIA process, and for this reason, it is good practice to introduce a certification scheme for EIA practitioners and consultants. At present, only South Africa, Botswana, Eswatini and Tanzania have a statutory requirement for certification of environmental assessment practitioners. Angola, Lesotho, Mozambique, Namibia and Zimbabwe have put in place registration systems for EIA practitioners based on professional criteria, which also afford some degree of quality control. Mauritius and Zambia require EIA consultants and their qualifications to be sent to the authorities for approval before commencing the EIA, affording a lower level of quality control that hinges on the accuracy of the information provided by the consultants. The lowest level of quality assurance is provided in DRC and Malawi, where the environmental agency has a list of approved consultants. In Comoros and Madagascar there is no certification or registration system for EIA practitioners. There is, therefore, little control over the professionalism and conduct of EIA consultants in the region.

Policy approaches to promote green investment

Uncertainty and unpredictability are among the greatest barriers to green investment. Too often the reason governments fail to attract green investment is due to the lack of an enabling environment for investment. Green investors are no different than any other in requiring a stable, predictable, and transparent investment environment in which to identify bankable projects. Thus, efforts to mobilise green investment will fail to meet their intended target unless governments ensure a regulatory climate that provides investors with fair treatment and confidence in the rule of law. The widely accepted features of this enabling environment are detailed in the OECD Policy Framework for Investment (PFI) which helped to inform SADC's own Investment Policy Framework.

At the same time, openness, stability, and fair treatment are not enough to channel private investment towards green growth and decarbonisation objectives. In other words, policies conducive to FDI will not automatically result in a substantial increase in green or climate-aligned FDI. Policymakers will also need to improve specific enabling conditions for green investment by developing policies and regulations that systematically internalise the cost of environmental externalities like carbon emissions. Targeted financial, technical and information support can also help address market failures reduce the competitiveness of climate-aligned investments.

Stimulating investment in green technologies

Private investors do not internalise the positive spillovers of low-carbon investments and are likely to under-invest in related technologies and skills compared to socially optimal levels. Targeted financial and technical support by the government is therefore warranted but must be transparent, time-limited and subject to regular review. Studies have shown that the variations in the cost-effectiveness of these technology support policies depend on the country context rather than on the specific tool used. In general, government support should decrease over time as the technology matures (OECD, 2022[11]). As noted previously, FDI in renewable energy is picking up in some SADC countries, but still considerably lags behind FDI in fossil fuels overall. Targeted measures to accelerate investments in the renewable energy sector can be an effective way to decarbonise the region and promote green growth.

Many SADC Member States have put in place incentives for renewable energy products and technologies. The most widely used forms of financial support include subsidies and grants for electrification programmes, tax exemptions on renewable energy equipment and generation, and tariff-based schemes like feed-in-tariffs (FiTs), public auctions and net-metering schemes (Table 5.5). Only South Africa has developed a carbon offset market since 2005, and has recently introduced a carbon tax to curb GHG emissions across sectors (Box 5.1).

Box 5.1. South Africa's carbon tax and offset market

Carbon pricing instruments (e.g. carbon tax) internalise the climate costs of carbon emissions and provide a technology-neutral case for low-carbon investment and consumption. Carbon offset markets allow companies to reduce the volume of taxable emissions by investing in specific projects or activities that reduce, avoid, or sequester emissions, and are developed and evaluated under specific methodologies and standards, which enable the issuance of carbon credits. Combining carbon offset markets and carbon pricing provides incentives for emissions abatement where it can be done at least cost, and also supports investment into the innovation required to lower the cost of emerging climate technologies. However, setting the carbon price too low results in little incentive to invest in carbon abatement.

South Africa introduced a carbon tax in June 2019, as one of the mix of measures for supporting climate change mitigation action. A key design feature of the carbon tax is the carbon offset allowance which provides flexibility to firms to reduce their carbon tax liability by either 5% or 10% of their total GHG emissions by investing in specific projects that are eligible for the issuance of carbon credits. The carbon offset system seeks to encourage GHG emission reductions in sectors or activities that are not directly covered by the tax, like public transport, agriculture, forestry and other land use, and waste. The new draft framework seeks to keep the domestic market in line with international standards which must be measurable, permanent, independently verifiable, unique and traceable.

Placing an adequate price on GHG emissions is of fundamental relevance to internalise the external cost of climate change in the broadest possible range of economic decision making and in setting economic incentives for clean development. There are, however, concerns that South Africa's current price on carbon is not enough to significantly contribute to reductions. According to the WWF, the current effective rate, paid once all allowances are taken into account, is equivalent to only 0.1-0.5% of the turnover of the highest emitters and will not be sufficient to meaningfully curb emissions. Moreover, the carbon tax rate was set to increase annually by inflation plus 2% until 2022, and annually by inflation, thereafter, meaning that the carbon tax no longer increases in real terms. Further raising the carbon tax and redistributing the revenues to lower-income households and help deliver a just transition.

Source: OECD (2022[14]); Republic of South Africa (2022[15]); WWF (2018[16])

The most widely used tax incentives to promote renewable energy include import tax and VAT exemptions on related machinery and equipment, provided by the majority of SADC countries. Four SADC Members (Mauritius, Seychelles, South Africa, and Zambia) also provide accelerated depreciation allowances on capital investment, which have the advantage of naturally providing diminishing fiscal benefits as an investment project matures. Angola, Mozambique and Zimbabwe offer corporate income tax (CIT) reductions or exemptions for a predefined period of time, which are potentially very costly in terms of forgone revenues. The same three countries simultaneously offer similar CIT tax reductions for investments in fossil fuels, eroding the tax base and reducing the ultimate effectiveness of efforts to promote clean energy investment. A similar misalignment is observed in Madagascar, Zambia and South Africa, where fossil fuels and renewable energy enjoy comparable tax allowances. In addition, many of these countries subsidise fossil fuel consumption either explicitly or implicitly, hampering the effectiveness of climate policies more generally (Box 5.2). These countries would benefit from categorising green and non-green activities according to emerging taxonomies and phasing out or scaling down financial and fiscal incentives granted to non-green activities, while implementing more targeted measures to ensure energy access and affordability.

Tariff based schemes like renewable energy FiTs and auctions have become an integral part of policy instruments to promote renewable energy investment in Southern Africa, and are provided by all SADC Members with the exception of DRC and Comoros. These instruments reduce the risk of private investments by guaranteeing a predetermined price (or tariff) for the electricity generated for a predefined period of time. FiTs schemes have been put in place by nine SADC countries and are typically combined with guaranteed access to the grid for renewable generators. A key drawback of FiTs is that setting the right tariff is a complex exercise with the rapidly decreasing cost of the technologies, particularly in young markets where government capacity in the design of FiTs may be low and there may be asymmetry of information between regulators and companies. Indeed there has been evidence of limited effectiveness of the FiT scheme in Malawi (OECD, forthcoming[17]).

Public auctions have the advantage of overcoming such informational asymmetries and promoting cost efficiency by allowing for a market-based and competitive determination of tariffs. This has led a number of SADC countries including Botswana, Madagascar, Mauritius, Seychelles, and Zimbabwe to opt for auctioning renewable capacity to determine the price of the FiT. While auctions are well-suited for established projects, they transfer higher risk to investors, and a number of SADC countries (Malawi, Namibia, South Africa, Zambia) opt for a hybrid approach combining FiTs and auctions.

Net metering is a billing mechanism that credits solar energy system owners for the electricity they add to the grid. As such, net metering schemes can be a vital policy option to encourage community-based small scale renewable energy producers, while also encouraging energy efficiency. Growing populations and increasing shares of SMEs in Southern Africa have amplified the demand for small-scale decentralised renewable energy projects. South Africa and Namibia were the first countries to use net-metering schemes, but they have now been adopted by ten SADC countries.

Table 5.5. Financial support for renewable energy

	Grants & loans	Tax incentives	Tariff-based schemes	Carbon markets	Taxes on energy use
AGO		CIT, Import tax	FiT, Net-metering		
BWA	National PV Rural Electrification Programme		Auctions		
COD	National Electrification Fund	Import tax, VAT			
COM	PASEC	Import tax, VAT			
LSO		Import tax, VAT	FiT, Net-metering		
MDG		Tax allowance, Import tax, VAT	Auctions		
MOZ		CIT, Import tax, VAT	FiT, Net-metering		
MUS	Technology & Innovation Scheme, Energy Scheme for SMEs	Accelerated depreciation	FiT 2010 (ended 2012), Auctions, Net-metering		
MWI	Rural Electrification Fund	Import tax, VAT	FiT, Auctions, Net-metering		Vehicle Tax
NAM			FiT 2015, Auctions, Net-metering	Under development	
SWZ					
SYC	SEEREP, SME Laon, PV rebate, Solar Cooling Storage Project	Accelerated depreciation, VAT	Auctions, Net-metering		
TZA	TEDAP, SREP	Import tax, VAT	FiT, Net-metering		
ZAF	REFSO, GEF Special Climate Change Fund	Accelerated depreciation, Import tax	FiT, Auctions, Net-metering	Carbon market since 2005	Fuel Levy, Carbon Tax, Environmental Levy
ZMB		Accelerated depreciation, Import tax,	FiT, Auctions		

		VAT			
ZWE		CIT, Import tax, VAT	Auctions, Net-metering		

Source: OECD FDI Qualities Mapping

Box 5.2. Reforming fossil fuel subsidies to align incentives with climate goals

Overall, fossil fuels remain highly subsidised in Southern Africa, with total explicit and implicit subsidies amounting to USD 62 billion in 2020, and projected to rise in subsequent years (IMF, 2023[18]). The level of subsidises varies considerably across countries, reaching as high as 16% and 14% of GDP in South Africa, and Angola, respectively, and lower than 2% of GDP for the majority of SADC countries. The majority of countries subsidies petroleum products, albeit to varying degrees, although coal still dominates subsidised fuels in South Africa, Botswana, Zimbabwe and Malawi. Following the surge in fuel prices since the onset of the COVID-19 pandemic and exacerbated by the war in Ukraine, subsidy levels are set to rise with fuel prices, which may reduce government capacity to promote clean energy.

Governments may resort to more targeted tools than subsidies on energy use to improve energy access and affordability. Phasing out subsidies could free up public funds for targeted support to low-income groups to ensure that vulnerable groups, which also tend to be those that are disproportionately affected by climate change, will be able to access clean and affordable energy (OECD, 2021[59]). However, potential adverse social impacts of phasing out the subsidies must be taken into consideration in order to deliver a just and green transition. Adequate compensation and support measures for those affected by subsidy reform should be put in place.

Figure 5.5. Fossil fuel subsidies in SADC

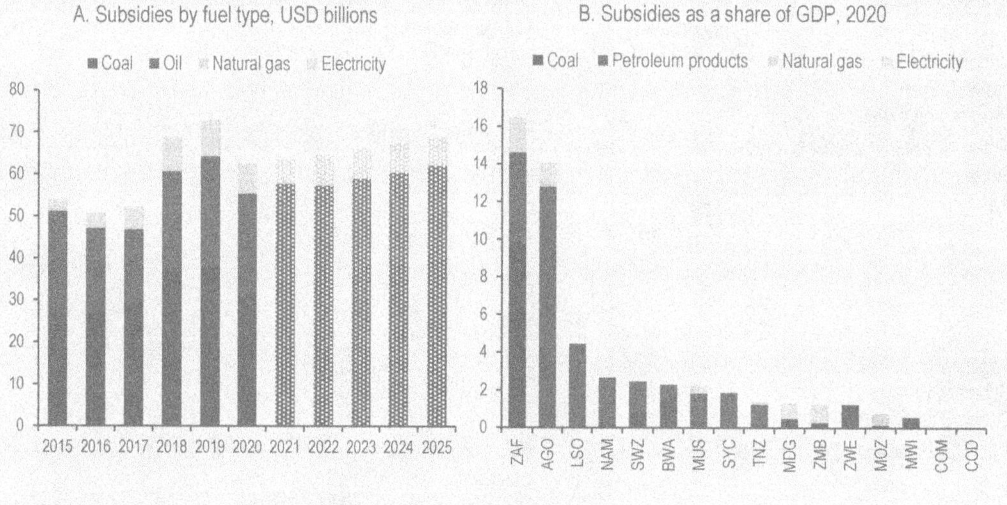

Note: Time series in constant 2021 prices; values from 2021 to 2025 are projections.
Source: Authors based on IMF Climate Change Indicators (2023[18]) https://climatedata.imf.org/

Building green capabilities and addressing informational barriers to green investment

Technical support is a useful tool for reducing the environmental footprint of investments, building capabilities related to green technologies, and promoting green innovation and spillovers. The majority of SADC countries offer technical support to develop renewable energy capabilities, in particular of workers, often delivered in partnership with development co-operation agencies (Table 5.6). For instance, the Southern African Solar Thermal Training & Demonstration Initiative (SOLTRAIN) is a regional capacity building programme implemented in Botswana, Lesotho, Mozambique, Namibia and Zimbabwe, with financial and technical support from the Austrian Development Agency. Similarly, the Green People's Energy for Africa initiative aims to improve the conditions for decentralised energy supply in rural areas in Mozambique, Namibia, and Zambia, and is implemented by the Deutsche Gesellschaft fur Internationale (GIZ). Malawi and Tanzania also have dedicated renewable energy training and testing centres. Namibia, Seychelles, South Africa and Zambia additionally offer technical support to improve the energy performance of SMEs and facilitate technology transfer. These kinds of initiatives are particularly useful to promote spillovers from foreign to domestic firms and further accelerate the green transition.

Green technology parks, incubators and accelerators can also be tailored to support businesses in finding innovative solutions to reducing GHG emissions, and create green innovation hubs that attract talent and investors. South Africa is the only country in the region to have developed a variety of different types of green technology parks. The Atlantis Greentech Special Economic Zone (SEZ) in the Western Cape is a noteworthy example that makes use of a range of investment attraction tools, including streamlined investment facilitation, preferential land use, infrastructure provision, easy access to major transport hubs, and SEZ-specific customs and fiscal regimes. The Global Eco-Industrial Parks Programme (GEIPP), launched in 2020, seeks to transform traditional industrial parks into Eco-Industrial Parks by improving resource use and fostering industrial synergies in existing industrial parks in the country. Through this programme, South Africa is striving to develop the first zero solid-waste eco-industrial park in Africa, known as the Limpopo Eco-Industrial Park. The South Africa Renewable Energy Business Incubator (SAREBI), established in 2012, seeks to help energy entrepreneurs in the renewable energy and energy efficiency sectors to build scalable, profitable and sustainable businesses. By upgrading the capabilities and innovation potential of domestic industry, these parks and incubation facilities can heighten competitive pressures and encourage FDI spillovers that arise from imitation of foreign technologies and operating procedures.

Table 5.6. Technical and information support for green investments

MS	Technical support			Information support		
	Training & skills development	*Business & supplier development*	*Science & technology parks*	*Green promotion & facilitation*	*Public awareness campaigns*	*Disclosure, certification & labelling*
AGO					EELA campaign	EITI Standard
BWA	SOLTRAIN				EELA campaign	
COD					EELA campaign	EITI Standard
COM					EELA campaign	
LSO	SOLTRAIN				EELA campaign	
MDG					EELA campaign	EITI Standard
MOZ	SOLTRAIN, Green People's Energy				EELA campaign	EITI Standard
MUS					EELA campaign	
MWI	Testing Centre in Renewable Energy Technologies				EELA campaign	EITI Standard
NAM	SOLTRAIN, Green People's Energy	Concentrated Solar Power Tech Transfer			EELA campaign	
SWZ					EELA campaign	
SYC		Grid-connected Rooftop PV Systems project			EELA campaign	EITI Standard, SYC Sustainable Tourism Label
TZA	Renewable Energy Training Centre				EELA campaign	EITI Standard
ZAF	Green Skills Program, Solar Training, SOLTRAIN	Industrial Energy Efficiency Program	Atlantis SEZ, SAREBI, GEIPP, Limpopo Eco-Industrial Park	Atlantis SEZ, Greentech Guide, WISP Investment Prospectus	Illegal dumping awareness campaign, EELA campaign	National GHG Emissions Reporting Reg., Green Star Rating
ZMB	Green People's Energy Training, Green Jobs in Construction	Online Course on Green Tech for MSMEs, PDDREP Training for SMEs		Energy Sector Profile	EELA campaign, Keep Zambia Clean, Green and Healthy campaign	EITI Standard
ZWE	SOLTRAIN					

Source: OECD FDI Qualities Mapping.

In addition to technical support, information and facilitation services can help reduce informational barriers and asymmetries that lead to sub-optimal investment and consumption choices, and generally result in under-investment in green technologies. For instance, lack of awareness on the energy performance of household appliances leads to an inability of consumers to interpret the impact of energy prices on the operational costs of one product relative to another, meaning that price signals do not influence purchasing behaviour as expected. Measures to raise public awareness and understanding of energy and environmental performance, including information campaigns, product labelling schemes, certification and disclosure requirements can help alleviate these information barriers.

Environmental awareness raising campaigns focus predominantly on energy efficiency. For instance, the SADC Centre for Renewable Energy and Energy Efficiency (SACREEE) is responsible for implementing the Energy Efficient Lighting and Appliances (EELA) project in Southern Africa, to raise awareness about the benefits of energy efficient technologies through television, radio, social channels and outreach events. South Africa and Zambia also publish sector-specific guidebooks and green investment opportunities listings to overcome information barriers that might hinder green investments. In terms of voluntary disclosure and reporting, ten SADC countries have committed to strengthening transparency and accountability of their extractive sector management by implementing the EITI Standard, which can play an important role in building awareness of how the transition will affect extractive sector activities and revenues and in supporting the responsible and transparent production of minerals that are critical for a sustainable future. South Africa furth introduced a system for the transparent reporting of GHG emissions, which will be used to maintain a National Greenhouse Gas Inventory.

References

Browne, C., C. Kelly and C. Pilgrim (2022), *Illegal Logging in Africa and Its Security Implications*, https://africacenter.org/spotlight/illegal-logging-in-africa-and-its-security-implications/. [2]

CRED (2023), *EM-DAT: The International Disaster Database*, https://www.emdat.be/. [8]

Financial Times (2022), *FDI Markets: the in-depth crossborder investment monitor from the Financial Times*, https://www.fdimarkets.com/. [12]

IEA (2022), *GHG Emissions from Energy*, http://iea.org. [10]

IEA (2022), *Greenhouse Gas Emissions from Energy*, https://www.iea.org/data-and-statistics/data-product/greenhouse-gas-emissions-from-energy. [6]

IMF (2023), *Climate Change Indicators*, https://climatedata.imf.org/. [18]

ISS (2021), *Climate finance isn't reaching Southern Africa's most vulnerable*, https://issafrica.org/iss-today/climate-finance-isnt-reaching-southern-africas-most-vulnerable. [7]

OECD (2022), *FDI Qualities Policy Toolkit*, OECD Publishing, Paris, https://doi.org/10.1787/7ba74100-en. [11]

OECD (2022), *Pricing Greenhouse Gas Emissions: Turning Climate Targets into Climate Action*, OECD Series on Carbon Pricing and Energy Taxation, OECD Publishing, Paris, https://doi.org/10.1787/e9778969-en. [14]

OECD (forthcoming), *Africa's Development Dynamics 2023*. [17]

Republic of South Africa (2022), *South African Carbon Offsets Programme: Draft Framework for Approval of Domestic Standards for Public Comment*, https://www.energy.gov.za/files/esources/kyoto/2022/Draft-Framework-for-Approval-of-Domestic-Standards-for-Public-Comment.pdf. [15]

SBDC (2014), *Country profiles - Madagascar*, https://www.cbd.int/countries/profile/?country=mg. [3]

UNDP-OPHI (2022), *Global Multidimensional Poverty Index 2022: Unpacking deprivation bundles to reduce multidimensional poverty*, https://hdr.undp.org/content/2022-global-multidimensional-poverty-index-mpi#/indicies/MPI. [4]

University of Notre Dame (2022), "ND-GAIN Index", https://gain.nd.edu/our-work/country-index/matrix/. [9]

Walmsley, B. and S. Husselman (2020), *Handbook on environmental assessment legislation in selected countries in Sub-Saharan Africa*, Development Bank of Southern Africa (DBSA) and Southern African Institute for Environmental Assessment, https://irp-cdn.multiscreensite.com/2eb50196/files/uploaded/SADC%20Handbook.pdf. [13]

Wolf, M. et al. (2022), *2022 Environmental Performance Index.*, Yale Center for Environmental Law & Policy, http://epi.yale.edu. [5]

World Bank (2023), *World Development Indicators*, https://databank.worldbank.org/. [1]

WWF (2018), *Everything you didn't know and should ask about the carbon tax*, https://wwfafrica.awsassets.panda.org/downloads/wwf_carbon_tax_qanda_final.pdf?24601/Everything-you-didnt-know-you-should-ask-about-the-carbon-tax. [16]

6 Promoting and enabling responsible business conduct

This chapter highlights the importance of responsible business conduct (RBC) for the SADC region and presents the key elements of RBC. It then provides an overview and analysis of policies and initiatives relevant to RBC at both regional and national levels within SADC.

In recent years a combination of regulatory, political and market pressures have driven uptake of responsible business practices globally. In SADC, policy makers, civil society, and business have recognised the importance to strengthen responsible business conduct (RBC) at both regional and national levels. SADC institutions and governments have established frameworks and policies that can serve as a foundation to further promote and enable RBC. However, there is a discrepancy in the pace at which countries and businesses have moved forward with the RBC agenda. Gaps remain to implement and enforce policies, to develop government action plans in line with international RBC standards, and to enhance stakeholder awareness and business capacity to conduct due diligence.

Importance of promoting and enabling RBC for SADC

Terms such as Corporate Social Responsibility (CSR) and Business and Human Rights (BHR) have been used to reflect the expectation that businesses should consider non-financial impacts as part of their core business considerations, rather than treating them as add-ons. RBC is more specific in that it sets the expectation that all businesses, regardless of their legal status, size, ownership structure, or sector, should avoid and address negative consequences of their operations while contributing to sustainable development wherever they operate. This means that businesses need to consider impacts on people, the planet, and society, such as human rights, labour rights, environmental and corruption risks that may be caused or contributed to by their business activities, their supply chains, and their business relationships.

Enabling RBC is key to attract quality investment, foster trade, and ensure that business activities contribute to broader value creation and sustainable development. The importance of implementing and enabling RBC has gained international recognition from business, trade, and investment perspectives. Enterprises have confirmed that implementing RBC practices and considering risks beyond financial materiality can be beneficial for their business. For example, the implementation of due diligence and higher sustainability requirements has proven to make companies more resilient to external shocks and crises. In a response to an OECD firm-level survey on RBC in Latin America, 75% of firms indicated that responsible practices such as due diligence have helped them navigate the COVID-19 crisis, notably by mitigating risks (OECD, 2021[1]). Similar results were found in a global study conducted by the World Benchmarking Alliance (WBA, 2021[2]).

For the 16 SADC countries, RBC is particularly relevant due to the structure of their economy and their integration into value chains, which relies on the extractive and the agricultural sectors. These industries have the potential to generate significant revenues and employment opportunities, but they are also associated with significant RBC risks such as human rights abuses and environmental degradation.

Agriculture plays a significant role in the socio-economic development of most member countries in SADC. It contributes to 70% of employment, 13% of exports and 66% of the intra-regional trade value (SADC, 2020[3]). The sector relies on smallholder farmers, and particularly women in the crop, livestock, and fisheries value chains and is almost entirely based on informal labour in SADC (ILO, 2020[4]). It is highly vulnerable to risks such as food insecurity and climate change, especially given that 90% of the region's crop production such as maize, millet and sorghum depends on precipitation. Agriculture's contribution to GDP varies greatly among SADC Member States. In Botswana, South Africa, Mauritius, and Zambia, agriculture accounts for less than 3% of GDP. On the other hand, in Madagascar, Mozambique, and Malawi, it makes up more than 26% of GDP. Except for South Africa, which also produces wine and citrus fruits, SADC economies are generally at similar levels of agricultural development and produce comparable products such as grains (maize, wheat, and sorghum), nuts, and vegetables (SAIIA, 2021[5]).

The region's economy and exports are heavily focussed on its abundant natural mineral resources and extractive products. Southern Africa is home to half of the world's vanadium, platinum, and diamonds, along with 36% of gold and 20% of cobalt (SADC, 2020[6]). Oil, gold, platinum, diamonds, copper, and cobalt accounted for around 72% of the region's total exports in 2021 (OEC, 2023[7]). More than half of the world's cobalt is sourced in DRC, which multinational companies use to manufacture rechargeable lithium-ion batteries, electronic devices, and electric cars (ILO, 2019[8]). Moreover, copper, cobalt, and platinum, for instance, have rapidly gained importance in the world economy being indispensable for the climate and green energy transition. The extractive sector is therefore crucial to the region's economy, employment, and foreign exchange earnings.

The agricultural and mining sectors in SADC have been associated with adverse social and environmental impacts in the past. The agricultural sector in SADC is linked to pertinent RBC risks, such as deforestation, weak land tenure rights for women, and child labour (SADC, 2020[9]; WFP, 2021[10]). Child labour is also an issue in mining, involving extremely hazardous working conditions and exploitation such as in cobalt supply chains in DRC (ILO, 2019[8]). Another negative impact of the mining sector in SADC is the spread of lung diseases such as tuberculosis and silicosis. The incidence of tuberculosis among miners is three to four times greater than that of the general population, and 89% of miners are believed to have latent tuberculosis due to exposure to silica dust, poor living and working conditions, and co-infections (NEPAD, 2023[11]).

Implementing and enabling RBC is key for SADC to address environmental, labour, and human rights risks in the minerals and agricultural sectors and thereby improve market access opportunities. This importance is further reinforced by increasing regulatory expectations related to RBC. In Southern Africa these expectations are driven notably by regulatory developments related to RBC in key exports markets such as the EU. Moreover, the ongoing implementation process of the African Continental Free Trade Area (AfCFTA) and its Protocol on Investment (in particular Article 38 on CSR) represents a key opportunity to further leverage RBC given the projected increase of both intra- and extra-African trade in a single continental market (UNECA/ FES, 2022[12]).

In addition to improved export market access, strong RBC policies dealing with labour standards, tenure rights over natural resources, human rights, anti-corruption, and integrity can contribute to attract more and higher quality investment to SADC countries. An OECD survey on FDI decisions found that strong and effective laws governing RBC- related issues represented the area, which had the strongest positive effect on encouraging investment in foreign agri-food markets (Punthakey, 2020[13]). Regional panel data analyses have further found that African and SADC economies having companies with robust RBC practices including on anti-corruption tend to attract more FDI (Agyemang, et al, 2020[14]; Chamisa, 2020[15]).

Key elements of RBC

The three main international instruments on RBC

The three main instruments that have become key reference points for responsible business globally, are the OECD Guidelines for Multinational Enterprises on Responsible Business Conduct (the OECD MNE Guidelines), the UN Guiding Principles on Business and Human Rights (UNGPs), and the ILO Tripartite Declaration of Principles concerning Multinational Enterprises and Social Policy. These instruments are aligned with and complement each other in the following areas (UN; OECD; EU; ILO, 2019[16]):

- *Framework for all companies.* International RBC standards set the expectation that all companies, regardless of their size, sector, operational context, ownership, and structure, should avoid and address adverse impacts and contribute to the sustainable development of the countries in which they operate.
- *Common understanding of impact.* The instruments set out that the impact of business activities goes beyond the impact on the company itself and refers to the impact business activities may have on human rights – including labour rights – the environment and society, both positive and negative. The instruments establish a common understanding that enterprises can cause,

contribute to, or be directly linked to adverse impacts, and they provide a framework for how enterprises should avoid and address them.

- *Conducting due diligence*. Businesses should undertake due diligence to identify, prevent, and mitigate their actual and potential negative impacts and account for how those impacts are addressed. This process involves meaningful consultation with potentially affected groups and other relevant stakeholders.
- *Responsibility throughout the supply chain*. Responsible business covers not only impacts that a company may cause or contribute to through its own activities but also those impacts directly linked to an enterprise's operations, products, or services through its business relationships. This includes business partners, entities in the value chain such as subsidiaries, suppliers, franchisees, joint ventures, investors, clients, contractors, customers, consultants, financial, legal, and other advisers, and any other non-state or state entities.
- *Access to remedy*. As part of their duty to protect against business-related adverse impacts, states are expected to take appropriate steps to ensure, through judicial, administrative, legislative, or other appropriate means, that those affected have access to effective remedy when such abuses occur within their territory and/or jurisdiction. In addition, where companies identify that they have caused or contributed to adverse impacts, they are expected to address them by providing remedy, and they should provide for or co-operate in this remediation through legitimate processes.

The OECD MNE Guidelines on RBC are the most comprehensive international instrument on RBC, providing recommendations to businesses in all areas of RBC. The Guidelines are part of the OECD Declaration on International Investment and Multinational Enterprises, which has 51 adherent countries. These countries have set up a unique implementation mechanism, the National Contact Points for Responsible Business Conduct (NCP), which promote the MNE Guidelines and handle cases referred to as "specific instances" as a non-judicial grievance mechanism in case of alleged violations of the OECD MNE Guidelines. This mechanism is accessible for stakeholders worldwide. Any trade union, civil society organisation or community can file a complaint which involves companies headquartered in one of the 51 adherent countries (OECD, 2023[17]).

While no SADC Member States has adhered to the Guidelines yet, several cases have been filed with respect to RBC issues that have arisen in the region. Between 2001 and 2022, 47 specific instances have been submitted in relation to business operations in SADC host countries. Most of them concern the mining sector and are linked to employment and labour issues. An example of a concluded specific instance relating to business operations in the SADC region is summarised in Box 6.1.

Box 6.1. Specific instance submitted to the Dutch NCP

In December 2015, the Dutch NCP received a submission from three individuals involving Heineken, a Dutch multinational and its subsidiary Bralima operating in the DRC. The three individuals stated that Bralima had not observed the OECD MNE Guidelines in the dismissals of 168 former employees in the DRC between 1999 and 2003.

In its initial assessment published in June 2016, the Dutch NCP accepted the specific instance for further consideration. The NCP offered its mediation services which both parties accepted. The dialogue was conducted under the chairmanship of the NCP and resulted in an agreement between the parties. The NCP was asked by the parties to monitor these next steps to ensure an objective, neutral and due process. Heineken also indicated that it would draw up a policy, including guidelines, on how to conduct business and operate in volatile and conflict-affected countries.

In April 2022, the Dutch NCP published a follow up statement acknowledging that the company had made important progress in developing and implementing RBC policies within the Heineken Group. The NCP further noted that compliance with the corporate governance principles should continue to be part of an ongoing monitoring process within the Heineken Group. The NCP concluded that the agreement reached by the parties had been fully implemented.

Source: Former employees of Bralima & Heineken and Bralima, http://mneguidelines.oecd.org/database/instances/nl0027.htm

Risk-based due diligence

As laid out in the international instruments on RBC, due diligence stands at the heart of the implementation of RBC, which requires companies to identify, prevent and mitigate adverse impacts, and account for how they address these impacts. This process means considering risks not only to the company but also those that companies can cause or contribute to along the supply chain.

The OECD Due Diligence Guidance for RBC provides a six-step process for conducting risk-based due diligence that can be used by any enterprise, irrespective of its size, location, or industry. The steps include embedding RBC into the enterprise's policies and management systems, identifying and assessing adverse impacts, ceasing, preventing, or mitigating adverse impacts, tracking implementation and results, communicating how impacts are addressed, and providing for or co-operating in remediation when appropriate. The OECD also provides tailored recommendations for specific sectors, including agriculture, minerals, garments and footwear, and finance (OECD, 2018[18]).

Figure 6.1. The risk-based due diligence process and supporting measures

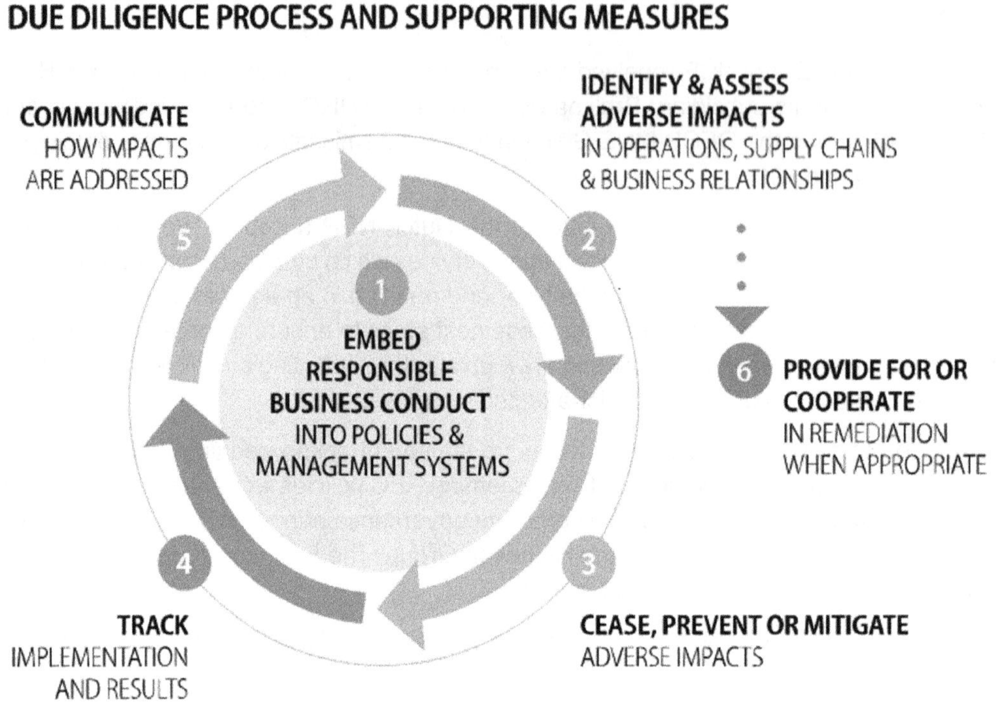

Source: OECD (2018[18]), http://mneguidelines.oecd.org/OECD-Due-Diligence-Guidance-for-Responsible-Business-Conduct.pdf

Governments worldwide are increasingly enshrining due diligence expectations in their laws. As of now, 75% of OECD countries have either introduced or are in the process of introducing some form of regulation that incorporates due diligence requirements, such as disclosure laws, conduct requirements, and product and trade bans. France, Germany, Switzerland, and Norway are among the first countries to have introduced comprehensive legislation that mandates companies to carry out effective due diligence processes. At the regional level, in 2022 the EU adopted a legislative proposal which aims to establishes mandatory due diligence that applies to both EU and non-EU companies, named Corporate Sustainability Due Diligence Directive (OECD, 2023[19]; EC, 2022[20]).

Policies and initiatives relevant for RBC in SADC

To promote the implementation of responsible business practices, it is necessary to have a supportive legal and policy environment at both national and regional levels. Governments have a role to play in creating conditions that drive, support, and encourage RBC. This involves establishing and enforcing legal frameworks in all relevant areas where businesses interact with people, the planet, and society, as outlined in the OECD's Recommendation on the Role of Government in Promoting Responsible Business Conduct (OECD, 2023[21]).

SADC policy frameworks to promote and enable RBC need further development

At the regional level, SADC has developed overarching, thematic and sectoral policies, which relate to RBC and international RBC standards. While these frameworks provide an important first step towards acknowledging and addressing RBC issues, SADC policy frameworks to promote and enable RBC need further development.

Overarching frameworks at SADC level

SADC has developed common policies and frameworks notably the SADC Protocol on Finance and Investment and the SADC Investment Policy Framework, which aim to create a favourable environment for investment in the region. These frameworks broadly refer to RBC and the use of international RBC standards, but do not provide further guidance on the promotion of RBC in different policy areas.

The SADC Protocol on Finance and Investment signed in 2006 aims to foster harmonisation of the financial and investment policies of the Member States. It requires all SADC countries to develop strategies for attracting and facilitating investment in their legislations. Annex 1 of the protocol regarding co-operation on investment includes Article 10 on "Corporate Responsibility". However, this article solely refers to the fact that foreign investors shall abide by the laws of the Host State and does not specify the scope or definition of corporate responsibility (SADC, 2006[22]).

The 2016 SADC Investment Policy Framework is based on the OECD Policy Framework for Investment and has become a reference instrument for investment-related reforms among SADC Member States. The framework directly refers to the promotion of RBC. SADC has also developed indicators to benchmark and monitor the Members States' progress in implementing the Investment Policy Framework in collaboration with the OECD, which includes RBC as one of the action areas (AUC/OECD, 2022[23]).

Moreover, SADC has developed a Model Bilateral Investment Treaty (BIT) Template in 2012, which aims to guide Members States through any given investment treaty negotiation. The second and updated version of the Template was published in 2017. It includes provisions that deal with the respect for human rights, the promotion of labour standards, the protection of the environment, or the fight against corruption without making direct reference to the OECD MNE Guidelines. For instance, Article 10 includes a common obligation against corruption. Article 13 further requires investors to conduct environmental and social impact assessments prior to investments. Article 15 sets out minimum standards for human rights, environment, and labour. It specifically refers to the corporate duty of investors to respect human rights and related international standards. Moreover, Article 22 establishes the mandatory obligation of states not to lower labour or environmental standards to attract investment (SADC, 2017[24]). According to publicly available information regarding the BITs of SADC Member States concluded since 2017, it remains unclear whether these RBC related provisions of the SADC Model BIT Template have been included in any recent agreement (UNCTAD, 2023[25]).

Further overarching SADC frameworks refer to issues related to RBC but do not make a direct link to business conduct. The SADC Vision 2050, for instance, includes the objective to achieve the sustainable utilisation and conservation of natural resources and effective management of the environment without referring directly to the role of the private sector (SADC, 2020[26]). Similarly, the SADC Regional Indicative Strategic Development Plan 2020-30 sets out the strategic objective to strengthen human rights but does not refer to RBC in this context (SADC, 2020[3]).

Thematic frameworks at SADC level

Putting in place and maintaining an appropriate legal and regulatory framework that is continuously implemented and effectively enforced in the areas of the OECD MNE Guidelines is key to enable RBC. SADC has developed a range of thematic frameworks, in this regard, in particular on human rights, labour rights, the environment, anti-corruption, and consumer protection (see overview in Table 6.1). At the same time, many of these frameworks do not refer to the role of business in relation to these issues or to the need to adopt responsible business practices in accordance with international instruments.

Table 6.1. SADC thematic policy frameworks related to RBC

SADC framework	Launch date	Content

Human rights		
Charter of Fundamental Social Rights in SADC	2003	Charter aimed at promoting and protecting basic human rights, freedom of association and collective bargaining, gender equality, children's rights, protection of health, safety, and environment.
SADC Protocol on Gender and Development	2008; revised in 2016	Protocol encouraging Member States to develop and implement legislation and policy to address gender issues.
SADC Regional Strategy and Framework of Action for Addressing Gender-Based Violence (2018-30)	2018	Framework to prevent, combat, and end all forms of gender-based violence.
SADC Declaration on Gender and Development	1997	Declaration to foster gender equality in the region by establishing policy and institutional frameworks within Member States, creating advisory systems to monitor gender-related issues, and establishing a Gender Unit in the SADC Secretariat.
Labour rights		
SADC Code of Conduct on Child Labour	2000, revised in 2022	Regional code of conduct to combat child labour.
SADC Protocol on Employment and Labour	2014	Protocol on labour rights including freedom of association and collective bargaining, equal treatment, working conditions, occupational health and safety, health care, children's rights.
Environment		
SADC Climate Change Strategy and Action Plan 2020-2030	2021	Regional plan to address and mitigate the environmental impacts of climate change.
SADC Forestry Strategy (2020-30)	2020	Strategic framework for national and regional co-operation to address challenges linked to the management of forest resources in the SADC region
SADC Green Economy Strategy and Action Plan for Sustainable Development	2015	Policy framework, strategy, and action plan to guide the integration of resilient economic development, environmental sustainability, and poverty eradication for green economy.
SADC Regional Biodiversity Strategy	2008	Strategy and guidelines to implement provisions of the Convention on Biological Diversity, and to foster consensus on key biodiversity issues and co-operation between Member States.
Anti-Corruption		
SADC Protocol against Corruption	2001; amended in 2016	Protocol to promote co-operation amongst Member States to develop mechanisms that prevent, detect, punish, and eradicate corruption in the public and private sector.
Strategic Anti-Corruption Action Plan for 2018-22	2018; currently updated for 2023-27	Framework for operationalisation of the SADC Protocol against Corruption
Consumer Protection		
SADC Declaration on Competition and Consumer Policies	2009	Protocol for Member States aimed at fostering competition, prevent unfair business practices, and establish a mechanism for consumer protection.

Regarding human and labour rights, certain overarching policies and commitments are of relevance to the promotion of an enabling policy environment for RBC. The Charter of Fundamental Social Rights in SADC and the SADC Protocol on Employment and Labour recognise basic human rights and labour rights building on the African Charter on Human and Peoples' Rights. Moreover, the 2016 Protocol on Gender and Development, among others, demands Member States to ensure equal access to employment and equal pay for work of equal value for all women and men in all sectors. The SADC Code of Conduct on Child Labour sets out the aim to create public-private and multistakeholder partnerships to encourage and promote responsible business and to prevent child labour in Article 6.8 (SADC, 2022[27]). At this stage, it is unclear from publicly available sources where the implementation process of this Code of Conduct stands.

With respect to the environment, SADC has several frameworks in place addressing various issues such as climate change and biodiversity protection, which mention the role of the private sector. The revised SADC Climate Change Strategy and Action Plan (2020-30) sets out objectives with respect to sustainable business conduct, for instance, identifying opportunities to reduce emissions, to improve waste management and to adopt sustainable techniques in the energy, agricultural and other key sectors. The SADC Forestry Strategy 2020-30 sets out the objective to put into place regional mechanisms to enable protection, sustainable management, and restoration of all forest types. It also identifies the conversion of forest land to agricultural areas, grazing land, infrastructure, and other land use as an ongoing challenge across SADC, and highlights the important role of the private sector and local communities in forest management (SADC, 2020[28]).

In relation to anti-corruption, the 2001 SADC Protocol Against Corruption aims to end all forms of corruption in both the public and private sector in all Member States. The Protocol refers among others to the importance of regional co-operation, participation of civil society, adequate access to information, and transparency in public procurement to prevent corruption (SADC, 2001[29]). Moreover, SADC is currently updating its Anti-Corruption Strategic Action Plan for the period 2023-27, which provides the framework for the operationalisation of the Protocol (SADC, 2022[30]).

Sectoral frameworks and initiatives at SADC level

In addition to thematic policies and frameworks relating to areas covered by the OECD MNE Guidelines, SADC has developed sector-specific policies which link to RBC, notably for the extractive and agriculture industries. Both sectors are key for the socio-economic development in SADC, yet also prone to human rights, labour rights, environment, anti-corruption, and conflict risks.

SADC has developed several policies and frameworks in the mining sector, which relate to responsible business practices. The SADC Protocol on Mining entered into force in 2000 and mandates Member States to harmonise their policies and procedures for mineral extraction. Its goal is to promote the mineral industry in Southern Africa and encourage private sector developments, including small-scale projects that empower disadvantaged groups in the mining sector. As outlined in Articles 8 and 9, Member States agreed to promote workers' health and safety, as well as environmental protection standards in line with internationally recognised standards. To facilitate these goals, the Protocol on Mining calls for the establishment of an organisational structure consisting of a Committee of Mining Ministers, a Technical Committee of Officials, and a Mining Co-ordinating Unit to oversee mining operations and ensure that applicable standards are upheld (SADC, 1997[31]).

In the agriculture sector, SADC has adopted the Regional Agriculture Policy in 2013 which is operationalised through the Regional Agricultural Investment Plan (2017-22) and the Food and Nutrition Security Strategy (2015-25). The Policy sets out the aim to improve sustainable agricultural production including through private sector engagement and investment in agricultural value chains (SADC, 2013[32]). The strategy also foresees to reduce vulnerabilities and risks related to RBC in the sector notably climate change, gender inequality, health, migration, and food insecurity (SADC, 2014[33]). At present, there is limited information available to the public regarding the implementation and monitoring process of this strategy.

Member States' national frameworks and initiatives relating to RBC

SADC governments have developed various policies and initiatives at the national level that address RBC issues and, in few cases, have started to integrate RBC instruments into their legal frameworks. However, comprehensive domestic regulation and specific action plans on RBC, for example, setting out due diligence expectations are not yet developed and adopted in the region.

SADC Member States have adhered to several international instruments in areas covered by the OECD MNE Guidelines, such as human rights, labour rights, the environment and anti-corruption. Table 6.2 illustrates that all SADC Member States have ratified key climate and anti-corruption related agreements such as the Paris Agreement, as well as the UN Convention against Corruption. However, gaps remain for the human and labour rights instruments, since several SADC countries have not adhered to all Core UN Conventions on Human Rights nor to all Fundamental ILO Conventions.

In addition to the adherence to international frameworks relevant for RBC, some Member States in SADC have started to develop national strategies to explicitly promote RBC. National Action Plans (NAPs) on

Responsible Business Conduct or Business and Human Rights can provide an important overarching policy framework for concrete state action for RBC, developed through inclusive stakeholder engagement. NAPs have been adopted by 30 countries around the world including Kenya and Uganda in Africa (DIHR, 2023[34]). They are policy documents setting out a common and evolving national RBC policy framework to protect against adverse human rights impacts by businesses (UNWGBHR, 2016[35]). In SADC, the development of NAPs has been limited so far. No Member State has yet published a NAP up to this point. Processes to develop a NAP are currently ongoing in four out of 16 countries: Mozambique, South Africa, Tanzania, and Zambia.

Table 6.2. Ratification of key international frameworks and development of National Action Plans

	Core UN Conventions on Human Rights	Fundamental ILO Conventions	Kyoto Protocol	Paris Agreement	Convention on Biological Diversity	UN Convention against Corruption	Extractives Industries Transparency Initiative	NAP on RBC / BHR
AGO	7/9	8/10	■	■	■	■	■	□
BWA	6/9	8/10	■	■	■	■	□	□
COM	5/9	8/10	■	■	■	■	□	□
COD	7/9	8/10	■	■	■	■	■	□
SWZ	7/9	8/10	■	■	■	■	□	□
LSO	9/9	9/10	■	■	■	■	□	□
MDG	8/9	8/10	■	■	■	■	■	□
MWI	9/9	10/10	■	■	■	■	■	□
MUS	7/9	10/10	■	■	■	■	□	□
MOZ	7/9	8/10	■	■	■	■	■	▣
NAM	7/9	8/10	■	■	■	■	□	□
SYC	9/9	9/10	■	■	■	■	■	□
ZAF	7/9	9/10	■	■	■	■	□	▣
TZA	6/9	8/10	■	■	■	■	■	▣
ZMB	8/9	10/10	■	■	■	■	■	▣
ZWE	6/9	9/10	■	■	■	■	□	□

Note: ■ = Ratified / member / developed; ▣ = Partially ratified/ under development; □ = Not ratified / not member / not developed.

NAP development processes have been driven mostly by civil society and non-state initiatives in the region. In Mozambique, the Ministry of Industry and Commerce expressed interest in leading the NAP process, however, it was initiated by the Mozambique Bar Association's Human Rights Commission in 2017. In South Africa, the initiative to develop a NAP is led by civil society and academia. The Centre for Human Rights at the University of Pretoria published a "Shadow" National Baseline Assessment of the Current Implementation of Business and Human Rights Frameworks in 2016. In Tanzania, the Human Rights Action Plan (2013-17) of the government tasked the Commission for Human Rights and Good Governance to develop a National Baseline Study on Business and Human Rights to support the NAP development. In Zambia, similar efforts have been led by the national human rights institution, the Zambia Human Rights Commission (ZHRC). The ZHRC published a National Baseline Assessment on Business and Human Rights in 2016 as well as a supplement to this assessment in the mining and agriculture sectors in 2020. As of March 2023, it has been reported that both the Tanzanian and Zambian Government has made a commitment to develop a NAP according to the most recent information available from the Danish Institute for Human Rights (DIHR, 2023[34]).

Aside from the limited number of NAPs, SADC Member States have put forward various national frameworks relating to RBC issues. Most Member States have established legislation with respect to labour and environmental issues in the mining and agricultural sectors. For instance, national mining codes in

SADC generally include overall provisions and required authorisations with respect to the protection of the environment. Moreover, SADC governments have legislations in place addressing forced and child labour in their countries and set up obligations for companies to conduct environmental impact assessments prior to investment projects. Some governments have set up initiatives with philanthropic purposes rather than relating directly to business impacts. For instance, Mauritius created a CSR fund based on a certain percentage of a business taxable income, which are used for programmes relating to the environment and sustainable development (MRA, 2021[36]). An overview of policies relating to RBC across SADC countries is listed in Annex 6.A.

Several governments have already started to promote the observance of the OECD RBC and due diligence instruments. Notably, the DRC has integrated the OECD Minerals Guidance into its legal framework covering tin, tungsten, tantalum, gold, copper, and cobalt via Ministerial Decree in 2011 (Government of DRC, 2011[37]). Moreover, the International Conference on the Great Lakes Region, which includes among others Angola, DRC, Tanzania, and Zambia has set up a regional certification mechanism for minerals, which requires traders to undertake due diligence aligned with OECD instruments (OECD, 2011[38]). In 2022, Mauritius submitted an official request to adhere to the OECD MNE Guidelines and started the adherence process in 2023, which would make it the first adherent country not only in SADC, but also Sub-Saharan Africa.

Several SADC Member States have also signed trade and investment agreements or partnerships, which include provisions relevant to promote and enable RBC. As the nature of trade and investment agreements evolves, they include increasingly provisions on the responsibility of business with respect to human rights, the environment and sustainable development, which has been driven notably by the EU trade and investment policies. The Economic Partnership Agreement (EPA) between the EU and the SADC EPA States (Botswana, Eswatini, Lesotho, Mozambique, Namibia, and South Africa) concluded in 2016, includes a chapter on Trade and Sustainable Development. This chapter refers among others to the commitment to multilateral environmental and labour standards such as the ILO conventions but does not refer explicitly to RBC (EU, 2016[39]). In addition, the EU and Angola concluded in 2022 the first-ever Sustainable Investment Facilitation Agreement. The agreement explicitly highlights the need to promote RBC and implement risk-based due diligence in Article 5.7 with a view to contribute to sustainable development. In this context, the agreement also supports the dissemination of the main international RBC instruments from ILO, OECD, and OHCHR (EC, 2022[40]).

SADC stakeholders' awareness of RBC

In addition to government policies in SADC, business and civil society are engaged in a range of RBC-related initiatives. However, many of these actions are still in their early stages and stakeholder awareness of RBC standards and due diligence approaches remains limited in the region.

Businesses in SADC are increasingly aware of the importance of RBC and engage in responsible business practices. UN Global Compact regional networks exist in Angola, Botswana, DRC, Mauritius and Indian Ocean Region (Comoros, Madagascar, Mauritius, Seychelles), South Africa and Tanzania. A total of 207 businesses participates in these networks, which work towards sustainable development in the areas of human rights, labour, environment, and anti-corruption (UNGC, 2021[41]). Moreover, national initiatives in SADC promote sustainable and responsible business practices such as the National Business Initiative in South Africa. The initiative is a voluntary coalition of over 100 South African and multinational member companies. It provides a platform for businesses to share best practices, collaborate, and develop solutions to social, economic, and environmental challenges (NBI, 2022[42]). Moreover, companies in minerals supply chains, for example in DRC, have been involved in various initiatives to implement due diligence processes over the last years. However, the advancement of these implementation programmes has been challenging so far (OECD, 2015[43]; OECD, 2019[44]).

Several civil society organisations in SADC are also leading initiatives to promote RBC. For example, the Legal and Human Rights Centre in Tanzania (LHRC) has set up the programme "Human Rights and Business", which seeks to promote responsible business among government and business in line with international RBC instruments including the UNGPs and the OECD MNE Guidelines (LHRC, 2022[45]). In Zimbabwe, the "Publish What You Pay" Coalition is a group of civil society organisations aiming to improve business transparency and accountability in the minerals sector (PWYP, n.d.[46]). In Mozambique, the Fórum da Sociedade Civil para os Direitos da Criança promotes children's rights and aims to reduce child labour via advocacy, capacity-building and partnerships with stakeholders including the private sector (ROSC, 2023[47]).

Several multi-stakeholder initiatives have started to reference and promote the implementation of the OECD due diligence guidance in SADC. For instance, in the context of cobalt mining in DRC, the Responsible Cobalt Initiative aims to address the risks associated with the cobalt supply chain through collaboration between business, the Government of DRC, civil society, and affected local communities. The initiative was founded by the Chinese Chamber of Commerce for Metals, Minerals & Chemicals Importers and Exporters and the OECD. It seeks to have downstream and upstream companies align their supply chain policies with the OECD Minerals Guidance (RCI, 2016[48]).

Although stakeholders in Southern Africa are becoming more aware of the importance of responsible business practices, gaps remain to collaborate across stakeholders and to build capacity of businesses to implement RBC practices. SADC governments can provide this support and guidance by creating a policy and regulatory environment for RBC and strengthening companies' capacity and ability to conduct due diligence. This is key to build more sustainable value chains, attract high-quality investments, and move towards sustainable development. Co-operation among governments, businesses, and civil society will be necessary to achieve this.

References

Agyemang, et al (2020), *Country-level corporate governance and foreign direct investment in Africa*, https://doi.org/10.1108/CG-07-2018-0259. [14]

AUC/OECD (2022), *Africa's Development Dynamics 2022: Regional Value Chains for a Sustainable Recovery*, OECD Publishing, Paris/African Union Commission, Addis Ababa, https://doi.org/10.1787/2e3b97fd-en. [23]

Chamisa, M. (2020), *Does Corruption Affect Foreign Direct Investment (FDI) Inflows in SADC Countries?*, https://doi.org/10.30871/jaat.v5i2.1873. [15]

DIHR (2023), *National Action Plans on Business and Human Rights*, https://globalnaps.org/. [34]

EC (2022), *Corporate sustainability due diligence, European Commission*, https://commission.europa.eu/business-economy-euro/doing-business-eu/corporate-sustainability-due-diligence_en. [20]

EC (2022), *EU-Angola Sustainable Investment Facilitation Agreement*, https://ec.europa.eu/commission/presscorner/detail/en/ip_22_6136. [40]

EU (2016), *Economic Partnership Agreement between the European Union and its Member States, of the one part, and the SADC EPA States, of the other part*, https://eur-lex.europa.eu/legal-content/EN/TXT/PDF/?uri=CELEX:22016A0916(01)&from=EN. [39]

Government of DRC (2011), *Note Circulaire numero 002/CAB.MIN/MINES/01/2011*, https://cdn.globalwitness.org/archive/files/library/note_circulaire_oecdguidelines_06092011.pdf. [37]

ILO (2020), *The Transition from the Informal to the Formal Economy in Africa*, https://www.ilo.org/wcmsp5/groups/public/---ed_emp/documents/publication/wcms_792078.pdf. [4]

ILO (2019), *Child labour in mining and global supply chains*, https://www.ilo.org/wcmsp5/groups/public/---asia/---ro-bangkok/---ilo-manila/documents/publication/wcms_720743.pdf. [8]

LHRC (2022), *Human Rights & Business*, https://humanrights.or.tz/en/post/resources-center/HRBReport21_22. [45]

MRA (2021), *Corporate Social Responsibility (CSR) Guide, Mauritius Revenue Authority*, https://www.mra.mu/download/CSRGuide.pdf. [36]

NBI (2022), *Introducing the National Business Initiative*, https://www.nbi.org.za/wp-content/uploads/2018/03/NBI-Brochure.pdf. [42]

NEPAD (2023), *TB in the Mining Sector in Southern Africa (TIMS)*, https://www.nepad.org/content/tb-mining-sector-southern-africa-tims. [11]

OEC (2023), *SADC*, https://oec.world/en/profile/international_organization/sadc. [7]

OECD (2023), *OECD Due Diligence Policy Hub*, http://mneguidelines.oecd.org/due-diligence-policy-hub.htm. [19]

OECD (2023), *OECD Guidelines for Multinational Enterprises on Responsible Business Conduct*, https://doi.org/10.1787/81f92357-en. [17]

OECD (2023), *OECD Recommendation on the Role of Government in promoting Responsible Business Conduct*, https://legalinstruments.oecd.org/en/instruments/OECD-LEGAL-0486. [21]

OECD (2021), *Survey Results on Responsible Business Conduct in Latin America*, https://mneguidelines.oecd.org/oecd-business-survey-results-on-responsible-business-conduct-in-latin-america-and-the-caribbean.pdf. [1]

OECD (2019), *Interconnected supply chains: a comprehensive look at due diligence challenges and opportunities sourcing cobalt and copper from the Democratic Republic of the Congo*, https://mneguidelines.oecd.org/Interconnected-supply-chains-a-comprehensive-look-at-due-diligence-challenges-and-opportunities-sourcing-cobalt-and-copper-from-the-DRC.pdf. [44]

OECD (2018), *OECD Due Diligence Guidance for Responsible Business Conduct*. [18]

OECD (2015), *Mineral Supply Chains and Conflict Links in Eastern Democratic Republic of Congo*, https://mneguidelines.oecd.org/Mineral-Supply-Chains-DRC-Due-Diligence-Report.pdf. [43]

OECD (2011), *The Mineral Certification Scheme of the International Conference on the Great Lakes Region*, https://www.oecd.org/investment/mne/49111368.pdf. [38]

Punthakey, J. (2020), "Foreign direct investment and trade in agro-food global value chains", *OECD Food, Agriculture and Fisheries Papers*, No. 142, OECD Publishing, Paris, https://doi.org/10.1787/993f0fdc-en. [13]

PWYP (n.d.), *Zimbabwe*, https://www.pwyp.org/pwyp_members/zimbabwe/. [46]

RCI (2016), *Responsible Cobalt Initiative*, https://respect.international/responsible-cobalt-initiative-rci/. [48]

ROSC (2023), *Áreas de Actuação*, https://www.rosc.org.mz/index.php/areas-de-actuacao. [47]

SADC (2022), *CODE OF CONDUCT ON CHILD LABOUR (REVISED)*, https://www.sadc.int/sites/default/files/2022-10/EN-%20Revised_SADC_Code_on_Child_Labour_30%20March%202022.pdf. [27]

SADC (2022), *Heads of SADC Anti-Corruption Agencies resolve to strengthen fight against graft*, https://www.sadc.int/latest-news/heads-sadc-anti-corruption-agencies-resolve-strengthen-fight-against-graft. [30]

SADC (2020), *Information Brief, Agriculture in the SADC Region Under Climate Change*, https://cgspace.cgiar.org/bitstream/handle/10568/110100/SADC%20Information%20Brief_FINAL.pdf. [9]

SADC (2020), *Mining*, https://www.sadc.int/pillars/mining. [6]

SADC (2020), *SADC Forestry Strategy 2020-2030*, https://amis-fis.jp/about-sadc/pdf/Draft_SADC_Forestry_Strategy.pdf. [28]

SADC (2020), *SADC Regional Indicative Strategic Development Plan*, https://www.sadc.int/sites/default/files/2021-08/RISDP_2020-2030.pdf. [3]

SADC (2020), *SADC Vision 2050*, https://www.sadc.int/sites/default/files/2021-08/SADC_Vision_2050..pdf. [26]

SADC (2017), *SADC Model Bilateral Investment Treaty Template*, https://www.civic264.org.na/images/pdf/SADC_BIT_template_final.pdf. [24]

SADC (2014), *Food and Nutrition Security Strategy 2015-2025*, https://www.resakss.org/sites/default/files/SADC%202014%20Food%20and%20Nutrition%20Security%20Strategy%202015%20-%202025.pdf. [33]

SADC (2013), *Regional Agricultural Policy*, https://www.inter-reseaux.org/wp-content/uploads/Regional_Agricultural_Policy_SADC.pdf. [32]

SADC (2006), *Protocol on Finance and Investment*, https://investmentpolicy.unctad.org/international-investment-agreements/treaty-files/2730/download. [22]

SADC (2001), *SADC Protocol against corruption*, https://www.sadc.int/sites/default/files/2021-11/Protocol_Against_Corruption2001.pdf. [29]

SADC (1997), *Protocol on Mining in SADC*, https://www.sadc.int/sites/default/files/2021-08/Protocol_on_Mining..pdf. [31]

SAIIA (2021), *Optimising Agricultural Value Chains in Southern Africa After COVID-19*, https://saiia.org.za/research/optimising-agricultural-value-chains-in-southern-africa-after-covid-19/. [5]

UN; OECD; EU; ILO (2019), *Responsible business: key messages from international instruments*, United Nations, OECD, European Union, International Labour Organization, Social Justice Decent Work, https://mneguidelines.oecd.org/Brochure-responsible-business-key-messages-from-international-instruments.pdf. [16]

UNCTAD (2023), *International Investment Agreements Navigator*, https://investmentpolicy.unctad.org/international-investment-agreements. [25]

UNECA/ FES (2022), *The Continental Free Trade Area (CFTA) in Africa – A Human Rights Perspective*, https://www.ohchr.org/sites/default/files/Documents/Issues/Globalization/TheCFTA_A_HR_ImpactAssessment.pdf. [12]

UNGC (2021), *Un Global Compact Africa Strategy 2021-2023*, https://ungc-communications-assets.s3.amazonaws.com/docs/publications/UNGC_Mobilising%20Business%20in%20Africa_2021_2023.pdf. [41]

UNWGBHR (2016), *Guidance on National Action Plans on Business and Human Rights*, https://www.ohchr.org/sites/default/files/Documents/Issues/Business/UNWG_NAPGuidance.pdf. [35]

WBA (2021), *COVID-19 and Human Rights, World Benchmarking Alliance*, https://assets.worldbenchmarkingalliance.org/app/uploads/2021/02/CHBR-Covid-Study_110221_FINAL.pdf. [2]

WFP (2021), *Climate Change in Southern Africa*, https://executiveboard.wfp.org/document_download/WFP-0000129015. [10]

Annex 6.A. National frameworks related to RBC

	Specific Frameworks/Policies Related to RBC
Angola	• **Extractive Sector: 2011** Law No. 31/11 approving the Mining Code Article 3: Preservation of the environment; Article 250: Provisions for Environmental Recovery • **Environment: 2020** Presidential Decree No. 117/20 approving the General Regulation for Environmental Impact Assessment and the Environmental Licensing Procedure • **Labour Standards:** 2018-22 National Action Plan for the Eradication of Child Labor (PANETI) (updated in 2022) • **Agriculture**: 2005 Lax No. 15/05 approving the Basic Agricultural Development Act Article 5: Farmer Protection; Article 9: Social Protections; Article 16: Protection of Forests • **Other:** 2018 Private Investment Law No. 10/18 Article 18: Specific Obligations; 2022 Sustainable Investment Facilitation Agreement between the European Union and Angola
Botswana	• **Extractive Sector: 1999** Mines and Minerals Act Part 9: Environmental Obligations • **Environment: 2011** Environmental Impact Assessment Act • **Labour Standards:** 2014 The Anti-Human Trafficking Act, No. 32 on child trafficking, forced labour, and trafficking • **Other:** 2020 A Code of Conduct for the Private Sector (Business Botswana)
Comoros	• **Extractive Sector: 2012** Law No 12-19/AU Petroleum Code Title 6 : Rights and Obligations • **Environment: 1994** Framework No. 94-018 on the Environment • **Labour Standards:** 2014 Law No. 14-034-2014 Concerning the Fight against Child Labour and Child Trafficking • **Other: 1995** Law No. 95-013 Code of Public Health and Social-Action for the Well-Being of the Population
DRC	• **Extractive Sector: 2018** Law No. 18/001 amending the 2002 Mining Code Article 42: Environmental and Social Instruction • **Environment: 2016** Ministerial Order No. 28/CAB/MIN/ECNDD/23/RBM/2016 setting the conditions for the approval of a consulting firm in environmental and social assessment • **Climate Change:** 2018 Ministerial Order No. 047/CAB/MIN/EDD/AAN/MML/05/2019 setting the approval procedure for REDD+ investments in the Democratic Republic of Congo • **Labour Standards:** 2009 Child Protection Code on child labour, forced labour, child trafficking, and slavery • **Other: 2016** Guidance on Corporate Social Responsibility: Mining Sector in Katanga
Eswatini	• **Extractive Sector: 2011** Mines and Minerals Act Part 7: Protection of the Environment • **Environment: 2002** Environmental Management Act • **Labour Standards:** 1980 Employment Act No. 5/1980 on forced labour • **Other: 2006** Prevention of Corruption Act
Lesotho	• **Extractive Sector: 2005** Mines and Minerals Act Part 9: Environmental Obligations • **Environment: 2008** Environment Act • **Labour Standards:** 2011 Children's Protection and Welfare Act on child labour and forced labour • **Other: 2016** National Investment Policy Section 6: Business Regulation and Taxation; 2021 Mohlomi Corporate Governance Code
Madagascar	• **Extractive Sector: 1999** Law No. 99-022 Mining Code Title 5 – Chapter 2: Environmental Protection • **Environment: 2015** Law No. 2015-003 on the updated Malagasy Environmental Charter • **Labour Standards:** 2007 Decree No. 2007-563 on Child Labour • **Other:** 2004 Law No. 2004-030 on the fight against corruption; 2015 Law No. 2015-014 on warranties and consumer protection
Malawi	• **Extractive Sector: 2018** Mines and Minerals Act Part 16: Protection of the Environment • **Environment: 2017** Environment Management Act • **Labour Standards:** 2015 Trafficking in Persons Act on child labour, child trafficking; and forced labour • **Other: 2004** Corrupt Practices Act
Mauritius	• **Environment: 2002** Environment Protection Act (amended in 2017) • **Labour Standards:** 2009 The Combatting of Trafficking in Persons Act on forced labour, slavery, and trafficking • **Other: 2016** National Code of Corporate Governance for Mauritius; 2016 Finance Act: Section 50L: CSR Fund; 2015 Code of Business Conduct (Financial Services Commission)
Mozambique	• **Extractive Sector: 2014** Mining Act No. 20/2014 Chapter 9: Environmental Management of Mining Activity • **Environment: 2005** Ministerial Order No. 198/2005 on Environmental Impact Assessment (EIA) • **Labour Standards:** 2014 Penal Code on child trafficking, forced labour, slavery, and trafficking • **Other: 1990** Fishing Law Title 3: Conservation Measures
Namibia	• **Extractive Sector: 1992** Minerals (Prospecting and Mining) Act Part 17: General Provisions • **Environment: 2007** Environmental Management Act • **Labour Standards:** 2007 Labour Act 11 on forced labour • **Other:** 2022-26 National Plan of Action for Small-Scale Fisheries
Seychelles	• **Environment: 2016** Environment Protection Act • **Labour Standards:** 1955 Penal Code on forced labour, slavery, and trafficking • **Other: 2010** Consumer Protection Act; 2016 Anti-corruption Act
South Africa	• **Extractive Sector: 2002** Mineral and Petroleum Resources Development Act Chapter 4: Mineral and Environmental Regulation • **Environment: 1998** National Environmental Management Act (amended in 2014)

	• **Labour Standards:** 1998 Employment Equality Act • **Other:** 2016 King IV Report on corporate governance; The Guidelines for Good Business Practice for South African Companies Operating in the Rest of Africa
Tanzania	• **Extractive Sector: 20**15 Tanzania Extractive Industries (Transparency and Accountability) Act • **Environment: 20**05 Environmental Impact Assessment and Audit Regulations • **Labour Standards:** 2009 Law of the Child Act on child labour and forced labour • **Agriculture**: 1997 Agricultural and Livestock Policy
Zambia	• **Extractive Sector: 20**15 Mines and Minerals Development Act Part 6: Safety, Health and Environmental Protections • **Environment:** 1997 Environmental Protection and Pollution Control (Environmental Impact Assessment) Regulations • **Labour Standards:** 1991 Constitution of Zambia on child labour, child trafficking, forced labour, and slavery • **Other: 20**10 Competition and Consumer Protection Act
Zimbabwe	• **Extractive Sector: 20**01 Mines and Minerals Act Part 9: Special Mining Leases viii) environmental assessment • **Environment: 20**16 Environmental Management (Prohibition and Control of Ozone Depleting Substances, Greenhouse Gases, Ozone Depleting Substances and Greenhouse Gases Dependent Equipment) Regulations • **Labour Standards:** 2013 Zimbabwe's Constitution on forced labour and slavery • **Other: 20**18 Public Procurement and Disposal of Public Assets Act; 2015 National Corporate Governance Code of Zimbabwe

www.ingramcontent.com/pod-product-compliance
Lightning Source LLC
Chambersburg PA
CBHW061223240926
51846CB00006B/1327